JUST IN TIME!

FUNERAL SERVICES

Cynthia L. Danals

Abingdon Press
Nashville

JUST IN TIME!
FUNERAL SERVICES

This book is printed on acid-free paper.

Library of Congress Cataloging-in-Publication Data

Danals, Cynthia L., 1960-
Funeral services / Cynthia L. Danals.
p. cm.—(Just in time!)
Includes index.
ISBN-13: 978-0-687-33506-0
1. Death—Religious aspects—Christianity. 2. Funeral rites and ceremonies. I. Title.
BT825.D33 2006
265′.85—dc22

2006012851

07 08 09 10 11 12 13 14 15 16—10 9 8 7 6 5 4 3 2 1
MANUFACTURED IN THE UNITED STATES OF AMERICA

In loving memory of Grayce

1995 to 2003

Contents

Introduction

This book is my gift to you. You may be a pastor, a chaplain, or someone seeking solace after a loved one has died. All of you have been in my prayers as I wrote this book. It has been my hope that all of you might find help in these pages.

As a hospice chaplain, it is my privilege to visit people who are dying. I'm also honored to assist families as they face the death of their loved ones. I enter their grief with them. It's like exploring an underground cave. I hand everyone a lantern and we descend. I walk around in the cave with them. Sometimes we encounter threatening creatures. At any moment, we sense that the cave may collapse on us. We may want to leave this place and never go back. But the deeper we can go, the more ease we can feel. We will be braver and a little closer to God.

The services in this book are designed to provide a word or a phrase, perhaps a whole paragraph, which could germinate a suitable funeral sermon. I've written three services for elderly persons, but I've also written stories of infants, children, youth, and younger adults, because in those situations, the shock and the heartbreak are most distressing. A pastor writing such a service may be at a loss for the words to describe the bitterness, the upset, or the sadness of such a loss.

Each of these services contains the story of someone who has died. The stories (or *contexts*) are fictitious, but I sense that each one of them has happened, sometime, to someone. I have personalized these so that you might be able to see the situation in your mind, perhaps identify the character with the one you know who has died. A scripture passage, a sermon, and two prayers follow each context. These may serve as an aid to one who is writing a funeral service, or they may be an inspiration to one who is suffering a loss. In either case, the sermon and prayers may be customized to address the needs of the bereaved.

For those experiencing the pain of a loss, my heart is with you. I have experienced such sadness. I never attend a wake or a funeral without a tissue ready. If you can find comfort in reading these stories of loss, then you have the beginning of wisdom. May God bless you as you continue to grow in God's image.

CHAPTER ONE

BIRTH AND NEWBORNS

MISCARRIAGE

Context

Melissa, a woman in your congregation, discovered that she was pregnant for the first time. She and her husband John were so full of joy that they announced it during the worship service. The whole congregation was swept up in happiness and anticipation.

After a few weeks, Melissa and John missed a Sunday, then two. You called them. Melissa had miscarried. When you met with them, Melissa said that she would like you to preach a ser-vice in memory of the baby for whom she and John had held so much hope. John agreed that such a memorial service would be healing not only for the two of them but alsofor the congregation.

Scripture

1 Samuel 2:1-10

Hannah prayed and said,
"My heart exults in the LORD;
my strength is exalted in my God.
My mouth derides my enemies,

because I rejoice in my victory.
There is no Holy One like the LORD*,*
no one besides you;
there is no Rock like our God.
Talk no more so very proudly,
let not arrogance come from your mouth;
for the LORD *is a God of knowledge,*
and by him actions are weighed.
The bows of the mighty are broken,
but the feeble gird on strength.
Those who were full have hired themselves out for bread,
but those who were hungry are fat with spoil.
The barren has borne seven,
but she who has many children is forlorn.
The LORD *kills and brings to life;*
he brings down to Sheol and raises up.
The LORD *makes poor and makes rich;*
he brings low, he also exalts.
He raises up the poor from the dust;
he lifts the needy from the ash heap,
to make them sit with princes
and inherit a seat of honor.
For the pillars of the earth are the LORD*'s,*
and on them he has set the world.
He will guard the feet of his faithful ones,
but the wicked shall be cut off in darkness;
for not by might does one prevail.
The LORD*! His adversaries shall be shattered;*
the Most High will thunder in heaven.
The LORD *will judge the ends of the earth;*
he will give strength to his king,
and exalt the power of his anointed."

Sermon

Hannah was a young woman with a dream. She had one request of God, that God would give her a child. When she bore a son, she dedicated him to God, naming him Samuel, for she had "asked him of the Lord." When she had weaned the boy, she took him, a skin of wine, some flour and a three-year-old bull to the priest. Before she gave away her son, she spoke a prayer of thanksgiving that began, "My heart exults in the LORD; my strength is exalted in my God."

The priest raised Samuel to be a priest. As an adult, Samuel would anoint David as king. He is one of the great priests of the Old Testament.

We never got to know John and Melissa's child. This child, a boy, was still forming in her womb when his spirit left his body. His parents hadn't yet seen his heart beating. They hadn't seen his lungs expanding and contracting. They hadn't yet counted ten fingers and toes. Yet they knew he was alive.

John and Melissa might have been able to tell what kind of character he would have. Would he have been insistent? Playful? Cheerful? Content? They couldn't really tell. They *did* know that they loved him already because they had asked him of God, and God had granted him to them.

From the moment of their son's conception, John and Melissa were parents. They were already providing him a safe home and good nutrition. They were full of excitement and expectation. They sensed God's favor. They had their work; they had each other; they had a home; and they had a child.

As much as they hoped for and desired this child, we would think that this pregnancy would have come to term, that the room the couple had prepared in their home would hold a strong, thriving baby boy, that the couple would bring him one day to be baptized, to be dedicated to Christian service, to the great joy of his parents and this congregation. But his life ended mysteriously, without warning. Now all of us are dealing with this painful loss.

Hannah had suffered loss. She went to pray in the temple. To the priest she explained, "I have been speaking out of my great anxiety and vexation all this time" (1 Samuel 1:16). Eli blessed her and sent her on her way. Soon after, she conceived.

Hannah dared to dream again. She offered Samuel to God to become a priest. God favored her with five more children. The Lord found her worthy of a high calling, mother of children.

In this congregation, there are many who have dared to dream again, who knew that God would grant their wishes for children, for career, for health, for home. We have asked these things of God, and God has favored us with generosity. Even as we experience the agony of this loss, we can still feel new hope and strength from the one who rallied the thousand as they fought the ten thousand, the one who caused water to flow from the rock, the one who gave us his son as a ransom for our sins, God Almighty, Creator of heaven and earth.

Prayer

Loving God,
  we praise you for the hope you gave us
  in the life of this child.
  We praise you for the excitement
  you created in these parents.
  We praise you for this, your congregation,
  steadfast both in joy and in sorrow.
  We ask your presence
  as we deal with our loss,
  that we may dare to hope,
  that we may continue to trust. Amen.

Supplemental Prayer

Gracious God,
  you give us beautiful dreams,
  bountiful hope,
  everlasting life.
  You are present in all of our relationships
    husband and wife
    parent and child
    friend and neighbor.
Let us hold to each other for strength.
Let us listen for your wisdom.
Make us your children,
and fulfill your great hope in us. Amen.

Premature Delivery

Context

Tad and Miranda are members of your community. They are related to some of your parishioners. They had been living together for two years when Miranda became pregnant. The couple hadn't anticipated having a child. The news spread among members of the community and the church. Their family members were reserved in their joy.

Because Miranda was in her late thirties, she began taking every precaution, from diet and exercise to the elimination of unhealthy habits. The couple started to consider marriage, and they approached you for counseling.

One night in her sixth month, Miranda began to experience complications. Tad rushed her to the emergency room. The couple discovered that Miranda had toxemia and dangerously high blood pressure, which might cause her to lose her life. Her doctor advised an emergency Caesarean section.

Miranda awoke the next day to find you and Tad at her bedside. Miranda had survived, but despite the best efforts of the surgeon, their baby had died. You listened as Tad stammered out the horrible truth. After they had held each other, sobbing, they asked you to provide a memorial ceremony.

The couple chose an ornate casket with pink satin lining and a ruffled white blanket. They named their daughter Ryleigh Suzanne. The funeral director himself delicately placed the tiny body on the cushion and covered her, then sealed the lid. The families of Tad and Miranda thought this an outrageous expense, but the couple felt justified.

Scripture

John 12:1-8

Six days before the Passover Jesus came to Bethany, the home of Lazarus, whom he had raised from the dead. There they gave a dinner for him. Martha served, and Lazarus was one of those at the table with him. Mary took a pound of costly perfume made of pure nard, anointed Jesus' feet, and wiped them with her hair. The house was filled with the fragrance of the perfume. But Judas Iscariot, one of his disciples (the one who was about to betray him), said, "Why was this perfume not sold for three hundred denarii and the money given to the poor?" (He said this not because he cared about the poor, but because he was a thief; he kept the common purse and used to steal what was put into it.) Jesus said, "Leave her alone. She bought it so that she might keep it for the day of my burial. You always have the poor with you, but you do not always have me."

Sermon

The story of Mary's anointing of Jesus is placed just before several chapters in which Jesus prepares his disciples for his death. When Judas objects to Mary's use of an expensive perfume, Jesus corrects him. Mary was preparing Jesus for his burial, with kind extravagance. It was important to Mary to give Jesus the same outpouring of love during his lifetime as she would during his death. After all, it had been Jesus who had brought her from a life of sin to the knowledge and the love of God.

And it was God who brought us Jesus. He came to us as a child, tiny and vulnerable. Mary and Joseph protected him. Angels heralded his birth. Shepherds attended him. Kings honored him. It would only make sense that Mary might prepare Jesus for his death in this lavish way.

Mary was one of the few who fully appreciated what Jesus would endure as the Son of Man. At this point in Jesus' story, the disciples were too worried about their loss to fully understand. Certainly, Judas didn't comprehend. He had his eye on the common purse. More for Jesus meant less for him. Judas spoke as though he actually had concern for the poor. Jesus knew better, but he treated Judas honorably.

Ryleigh Suzanne, daughter of Tad and Miranda, had the shortest of lives here on earth. The joy with which her parents anticipated her inspired the entire town. The preparations the couple made for her, the sacrifices, and the plans were made with excitement. The angels heralded Ryleigh's birth just as they had heralded the birth of Jesus. And she arrived as he did, tiny and vulnerable. Ryleigh, much to our sorrow, was far too fragile to survive.

And so we celebrate her life even as we mourn her death, with much finery. We give her everything possible in death just as parents give their children everything possible in life. We are anointing our children every day, with new shoes, new notebooks, new sports equipment, new clothes. Ryleigh will never need any of these things, so Miranda and Tad have anointed her with lovingkindness. They have prepared her for burial just as Mary prepared Jesus.

We don't know what Ryleigh would have been like. We don't know which of her parents she would have resembled more. We don't know the sound of her voice, for even her first cry was stifled. What we do know is that she was much beloved by her family, by her community, and by her God. I can tell by the love on our faces now, that we truly are a community that God has blessed with the spiritual gift of compassion. We are strong even in our weakness, even as Mary was joyful even in her sadness as she anointed Jesus' feet. May God bless us as we care for Tad and Miranda, and as we remember their child, Ryleigh Suzanne.

Prayer

Loving God,
you are all compassion.
You understand the loss of a child
because you lost your own son.
As we have prepared Ryleigh for burial,
so prepare our hearts for the days to come.
Bless us in our sorrow, we pray.
Amen.

Graveside Prayer

Gracious God,
you loved us before we loved you.
You have nurtured us through our childhood.
You have strengthened our faith.

Give us the courage to love one another
as you have loved us.
Amen.

Stillbirth

Context

Milo and Tatiana were expecting their first child. Even though Milo held a responsible position in his organization, he accompanied Tatiana to the many obstetrician appointments that would lead up to their child's birth. They meticulously cared for their baby girl.

In the twenty-fourth week of the pregnancy, Tatiana awoke in the middle of the night. Returning to the bedroom from the bathroom, she sensed that something was wrong. The child she was carrying was not moving.

She awakened Milo, who rushed her to the hospital. On the way, Milo called the Emergency Department to alert the medical team. Then he called the prayer chain at your church. Beside Milo in the passenger seat, Tatiana prayed for strength.

Tatiana was admitted immediately, examined, and taken to the obstetrics floor for observation. By 3:00 a.m., the grim truth was known. Their child's umbilical cord had wrapped around her neck. She had died in the womb.

Milo called you at 7:00 a.m. at home. He requested that you come see Tatiana. The couple had decided to name the child Cherise Mackenzie. They asked you to prepare a service of death and resurrection.

Scripture

Matthew 27:45-54

From noon on, darkness came over the whole land until three in the afternoon. And about three o'clock Jesus cried with a loud voice, "Eli, Eli, lema sabachthani?" that is, "My God, my God, why have you forsaken me?" When some of the bystanders heard it, they said,

"This man is calling for Elijah." At once one of them ran and got a sponge, filled it with sour wine, put it on a stick, and gave it to him to drink. But the others said, "Wait, let us see whether Elijah will come to save him." Then Jesus cried again with a loud voice and breathed his last. At that moment the curtain of the temple was torn in two, from top to bottom. The earth shook, and the rocks were split. The tombs also were opened, and many bodies of the saints who had fallen asleep were raised. After his resurrection they came out of the tombs and entered the holy city and appeared to many. Now when the centurion and those with him, who were keeping watch over Jesus, saw the earthquake and what took place, they were terrified and said, "Truly this man was God's Son!"

Sermon

Those who witnessed the crucifixion of our Lord Jesus Christ were in a state of confusion and agitation. They may not have known why he had to die. They may not have expected him to cry out his pain from the cross. They did not understand what he was trying to say. They were frightened by the darkening of the sky, the tearing of the temple curtain, and the reappearance of the saints who had died.

When God lost his son, he expressed his grief in dramatic ways. Rain poured from the skies. The earth shook with God's sobs. The saints rose in response. The righteous recognized Jesus' true identity, and their sorrow was profound.

We find ourselves in a similar situation. We are in a state of confusion and agitation. We expected Cherise Mackenzie to thrive. We expected her to emerge strong and healthy. We prayed for this couple as they sped through the night to the hospital.

Sadly, like those who witnessed Jesus' crucifixion, the situation was untenable. Like God, we watched as the unimaginable happened. Then the earth shook with our sobs. Tears ran down our faces and dropped on the pages of our Bibles. The medical team, the prayer chain, Milo and Tatiana—all of us were miserable in our powerlessness.

God has mercy on us. God knows what it is like to lose a child. Jesus, his arms outstretched on the cross, called out, "My God, my God, why have you forsaken me?" Any parents would move heaven and earth to save their child from illness or injury or death. God could not save Jesus. God watched his only son die in excruciating pain.

As we sit in our helplessness, God's love surrounds us. God has traveled the road to the cross. God has suffered the death of his only son. God has given his son so that we may be saved. God understands our anger, our disbelief, our sorrow.

When Jesus died on the cross, he entered eternal life. He showed us the way. He has greeted this baby girl, taken her in his arms, and introduced her to a heaven full of comfort, peace, and nourishment. He has marveled at her beauty. He has turned to the angels, and he has introduced her as Cherise Mackenzie, daughter of Milo and Tatiana. God smiled, knowing how much Jesus loves children, and joined him and the angels in adoring this child.

Cherise Mackenzie has received her reward. She is in heaven's care. She will never have to be hungry, thirsty, or in need. She will never get a bad grade on a spelling test. She will never endure illness. She will be in empathy with Tatiana and Milo, and devote herself to prayer on their behalf, responding to their mourning by asking God's care of them.

One day Milo and Tatiana will experience new warmth. We will all know a welcome peace in time. Then Cherise Mackenzie will rejoice with us, that God has heard our prayers and that we have heard God's promise, expressed through his son Jesus Christ, that he will never leave us or forsake us. Until then, let us hold on to each other and live in the hope of the resurrection.

Prayer

Compassionate God,
we are grateful for the life of your son Jesus Christ
and the hope of resurrection.
We thank you for Milo and Tatiana,

for their loving care of Cherise Mackenzie.
We thank you for this baby girl,
now safe in your care,
who is even now teaching us how to love
and overflowing your heart with prayers for us.
Amen.

Graveside Prayer

Gracious God,
we ask your care of us,
for we are overwhelmed with grief.
Our sense of loss is tremendous.
Help us in the coming days
to be conscious of your care
to be open to your lovingkindness
to see your face in those around us.
May we draw strength from you and your people.
Amen.

INFANT DIES IN SLEEP

Context

Joan and Timothy's family participated in every church activity, from Sunday school, to worship, to the annual Christmas pageant. With four children, two boys and two girls, aged three through eight, this couple was grateful for fun, low-cost activities that were also edifying.

When Joan discovered that she was pregnant with a fifth child, the couple rejoiced *and* despaired. While they were elated to welcome another child, they wondered how they would manage financially. Joan would have to take pregnancy leave once more from her job. Tim would also need to take time off to help with the children.

The baby boy arrived in September, and despite the worries, the family received him with delight. Since he would be the youngest baby boy born in the congregation by Christmas, the director of Christian Education asked Joan if she would allow him to play Baby Jesus in the pageant that year. Joan accepted the honor on his behalf.

One day, while she was still on pregnancy leave, Joan put Tommy down for an afternoon nap. As she watched him fall asleep, she thought of Baby Jesus, how he'd started with so little and had become Savior of the World. She relished that thought, then left the room to complete some chores.

The time came for Tommy to wake up, but since she hadn't heard him cry, Joan entered his nursery. He lay motionless. She picked him up. His nail beds were blue, and he wasn't breathing. She shouted for Tamara, her eldest, to call 911.

Tommy was dead on arrival at Children's Hospital. Tim arrived to find Joan curled in a fetal position, weeping. Later that hour, Tim would call to ask you to provide pastoral care and to arrange a funeral service.

Scripture

Matthew 2:16-18

When Herod saw that he had been tricked by the wise men, he was infuriated, and he sent and killed all the children in and around Bethlehem who were two years old or under, according to the time that he had learned from the wise men. Then was fulfilled what had been spoken through the prophet Jeremiah:

"A voice was heard in Ramah,
wailing and loud lamentation,
Rachel weeping for her children;
she refused to be consoled,
because they are no more."

Sermon

During Jesus' time, rulers often resorted to drastic means to stay in power. Herod had heard of the birth of a potential rival, and he was determined that a small child would not usurp his throne. He was so resolved that he committed one of the most heinous crimes in history, depriving scores of young mothers of their small children.

It is hard to imagine the depth of anguish these families experienced. For no good reason, suddenly, the children they had cherished were no more. Their friends and neighbors were also mourning their losses. The government, which may have seemed remote in the past, was now tyrannical. Little help was available, except from God.

God deals with us in our shock, our anger, our deep sorrow over our losses. God provides ways for us to express ourselves, people who draw us out, even moments of hope in the midst of agony. God gives us ways to mourn the loss of those we have loved.

Thomas Joseph was the fifth child of Tim and Joan. He was the youngest in a loving household teeming with energy and vibrancy. He contributed to this vitality with his lusty voice, which issued demands for attention and care. He responded well to good treatment and grew strong in his infancy. He was a joy to his family, who cared for him deeply, providing all he needed to thrive.

Unbeknownst to his parents, however, something was wrong within his body. No one in his family, not even his pediatrician, could have perceived it. All who cared for Tommy were blindsided by a mysterious illness that claimed his life silently, painlessly. He died in his sleep.

Like the children massacred by Herod, he was defenseless. Like the parents of these children, Joan and Tim could not have prevented his death. When the numbness of their shock gave way to anger and tears, they sought help from God, the same God who comforted the families of Bethlehem's slain children long ago.

It may be a long time before life feels right again for this family. It may be a while before they can speak the name of their child. The family will never forget Tommy. But one thing is certain. The Parent of us all, the Creator of the world, who gave us Jesus Christ as a tiny baby, is steadfast in his love, now and forever. God will respond with compassion to the needs of this family, because God, too, lost his child.

It was dark on the day Jesus hung on the cross, and at the final moment of his struggle with death, the curtain in the temple tore from top to bottom. God mourned Jesus' death and wept in misery. When Jesus ascended to heaven, God had finished crying. He greeted his son with his arms wide open, and they embraced. Heaven's gates shook with the sound of their laughter. All was bliss.

Tommy has been reunited with God. But like the disciples Jesus left behind, we are wondering what to do with ourselves, how to manage this flood of feelings, how to respond to the needs of this family. God has promised help on earth, and a home in heaven. May we hold fast to these promises as we grow in God's image.

Prayer

Almighty God,
we praise you for your steadfast love.
We rely on your strength
to bolster us for the days ahead.
Guide us, God,
and help us bless each other with compassion.
Amen.

Graveside Prayer

Gracious God,
we are your children,
brimful of your grace
and strong in our faith.
Empower us to live
in service to you,
bringing honor to your name.
Amen.

INFANT IS FATALLY INJURED

Context

Ruth and Alex lived in an old house in a multicultural neighborhood. They had won the right to purchase the house for a penny in a citywide essay contest. The couple had taken time off work to begin renovations. They were able to shore up the first floor and complete the electrical work. When they returned to their jobs, they finished the rest of the house a room at a time. They hosted an open house and invited their neighbors.

By this time, Ruth was pregnant with the couple's first child. One of their neighbors threw a baby shower. This provided the furniture and other provisions for the nursery that the couple had begun to decorate. Nothing could have pleased the couple more.

The baby was born, a boy named Anthony Ross. Ruth and Alex were the most careful of parents, taking every precaution to ensure their child's safety and comfort. One night, Alex had a cold, so he slept downstairs on the couch in the living room. Ruth slept upstairs in the bedroom next to the nursery. A light sleeper, she was awakened by a sound she couldn't identify. She made her way downstairs to the living room. Just as she stepped onto the landing, the kitchen burst into flame due to a short in the wiring.

Ruth screamed to Alex, who grabbed the cordless phone and pulled Ruth outside. Alex called the fire department, which dispatched a pumper immediately. In the meantime, Ruth decided she would rescue Tony. By this time, some of the neighbors had arrived. They did their best to hold back the distraught parents, telling them to wait for the firefighters. The pumper arrived in five minutes, and the firefighters made several attempts to rescue the baby. By the time they were able to reach the child, he had died of smoke inhalation and had been badly burned.

Scripture

Genesis 21:14-19

So Abraham rose early in the morning, and took bread and a skin of water, and gave it to Hagar, putting it on her shoulder, along with the child, and sent her away. And she departed, and wandered about in the wilderness of Beer-sheba.

When the water in the skin was gone, she cast the child under one of the bushes. Then she went and sat down opposite him a good way off, about the distance of a bowshot; for she said, "Do not let me look on the death of a child." And as she sat opposite him, she lifted up her voice and wept. And God heard the voice of the boy; and the angel of God called to Hagar from heaven, and said to her, "What troubles you, Hagar? Do not be afraid; for God has heard the voice of the boy where he is. Come, lift up the boy and hold him fast with your hand, for I will make a great nation of him." Then God opened her eyes and she saw a well of water. She went, and filled the skin with water, and gave the boy a drink.

Sermon

The story of Ishmael and Hagar is one of the most tragic in the Old or New Testaments. A mother and her child are cast away, and then the mother is forced to abandon her child when their provisions run out. She is resigned. She is desperate. Then God intervenes. God fulfills Hagar's immediate need and casts a vision for the child's future.

In the case of Ruth and Alex, the immediate need is different, but God's compassion for them is the same. Despite the desperation in any situation, God is still present, working within the family and within those who surround the family to restore all to wholeness.

Despite the couple's protests, several neighbors advised them against running back into the house to rescue their son. Two strong men stepped forward to restrain Ruth, whose maternal instincts were compelling her to risk her own life to save Anthony Ross. Alex saw the sense in staying outside, and gently coaxed Ruth to wait for the professionals.

After the firefighters had arrived, and after they had found Anthony Ross, an elderly couple shuffled across the street with two cups of hot cocoa, which Alex and Ruth accepted. A neighbor volunteered to drive the couple with their baby to Children's Hospital. Another offered accommodations for the night. God was working through the couple's neighbors to bring peace and comfort amidst the tragedy.

While the neighbors provided help for the immediate needs, God was getting ready to receive Anthony Ross. God lifted up the child. God cared for the child's needs. God healed him from the effects of the smoke inhalation and the burns from the fire. Anthony Ross received a new body in heaven, and is now clothed in righteousness. God is cherishing him, just as his parents cherished him.

But God is also cherishing Tony's parents, Ruth and Alex. God is opening his everlasting arms and inviting them to press themselves to his bosom. God wants them to avail themselves of him in the coming weeks and months, just as the neighbors want Ruth and Alex to come to them for nurture and support. My arms are open too. We all are willing to help, through the power of the God who has sustained us through the many heartrending situations that we have experienced.

May we all love our neighbor as God has loved us.

Prayer

Loving God,
We are saddened by the loss of Anthony Ross.
We ask for your help in caring for his parents,
Alex and Ruth.
We ask that we might be for them
as a well, brimful, in the desert. Amen.

Graveside Prayer

Gracious God,
We are your hands and feet on earth.
You have given us a wonderful couple

to support and nurture.
May we indeed fulfill your great commandment
to love our neighbors as ourselves. Amen.

Infant Dies in Neonatal Intensive Care Unit

Context

Juniper "June" Grace was the name of a baby girl born prematurely. She weighed two pounds and one-half ounce when the world welcomed her. By the time she had taken her second shallow breath, the surgical staff had her on a respirator in an incubator. Tubes and needles obscured her parents' view of her as they sat at her side in the neonatal intensive care unit.

Gloria, her mother, had had a difficult pregnancy. She and her husband John had spent more than a few anxious nights wondering whether or not to go to the hospital. Gloria's doctor, Morgan, advised her to call whenever she was unsure. The doctor had met the couple three times in the emergency room after midnight.

The most recent bout had been life threatening. Gloria contracted toxemia and a Caesarian-section was necessary. Morgan accompanied Gloria to the operating room, and then returned to the waiting room to console John. After the baby was born, Morgan made daily trips to the neonatal intensive care unit to check on June's progress. After two-and-a-half weeks, June died in a nurse's hands while Morgan was visiting. Morgan called you to offer pastoral care to the couple, who then asked you to officiate at a memorial service for their child.

Scripture

John 14:15-17

"If you love me, you will keep my commandments. And I will ask the Father, and he will give you another Advocate, to be with you

forever. This is the Spirit of truth, whom the world cannot receive, because it neither sees him nor knows him. You know him, because he abides with you, and he will be in you."

Sermon

In the Gospel according to John, Jesus gathered his disciples together for one last time to instruct them. He was about to die on the cross, and he was concerned that they might be discouraged enough after he died to abandon the ministry they had begun. He knew they would need some additional help and reassurance. He told them about the Holy Spirit, who would come in his place to advocate for the disciples, interpreting the scriptures, perfecting their prayers, and reminding them of everything Jesus had taught.

The disciples went on from that moment to do greater works in Jesus' name. Because he left them with help and inspiration, they were able to face down judges, high priests, and angry throngs, speaking the right words at the right time. The Holy Spirit lived on in them, as the Spirit lives on in us, empowering us even when we're too discouraged to continue with our lives.

God does not want to leave us desolate. God may or may not have known how long June would live, but God knew John and Gloria would do everything possible for her as her parents. And June knew her parents. She felt the familiarity of their touch even through the gloves they had to wear to hold her. She wriggled in pleasure as they held her. She even smiled a few times. Gloria is sure she saw June laugh at her.

God didn't want to leave June's parents alone. God sent a wonderfully vigilant doctor, Morgan, to keep her parents informed and to comfort them. God sent the nurses and doctors at her hospital to monitor her and to respond to June's needs. God sent a caring extended family, who set up an information network for Gloria so that she only had to tell one person about her daughter's progress each time she had news to report. God sent our congregation to care for her parents after June passed away.

Finally, God sent the Holy Spirit, which will comfort the couple now and for years to come. The Holy Spirit will abide in them, confirming their hope, giving them peace, and helping them to understand all that God asks of them through the scriptures. God's Spirit will also inform those of us who are caring for Gloria and John, helping us work with them to discern their needs. We will walk with them, until they come to the place, at last, where they may walk by themselves, still broken, but stronger, able, perhaps, to help others through a similar difficulty.

After the disciples witnessed Jesus' death on the cross, all was lost for them. Even though Jesus had given them good instruction, none of it had been written down. They needed someone to remind them, someone to renew them, someone to stir the cinders of the hope they still had. Jesus reappeared to the disciples himself to reassure them, by some accounts many times. He knew that he couldn't stay with them, however, so he sent the Holy Spirit to comfort and guide them, to remind them of everything he had taught them.

May we all leave this place with the power of the Holy Spirit, ready to do God's will in Jesus' name.

Prayer

Loving God,
we are grateful for the life of Juniper Grace,
for all of the care we were able to give,
and for all of the love you've shown through us.
By the power of the Holy Spirit,
may we grow in strength and in love
that we may continue to offer your care to John and Gloria. Amen.

Graveside Prayer

Gracious God,
you give us power and love.
May we also give your power and love in abundance
to all who ask it of us.
By the power of the Holy Spirit,
may we fulfill the need of many,

so that when you call us to your home
yours will be a familiar voice. Amen.

Infant Dies Due to Mistreatment

Context

Theodora "Teddy" Lillian, six months old, was the fifth child of Darla and Bob. The couple had been surprised to become pregnant in their forties. Their other children were teenagers. Their sons—Bob Jr., eighteen, and Mark, sixteen—were ambivalent, and their daughters—Danielle, fourteen, and Delilah, twelve—were unenthused. The girls had been looking forward to the day the boys moved out so that they could take over their bedrooms. Now the boys both moved into one room to allow Bob Sr. to decorate the other as a nursery. All of the children had wanted a little more of their mother's attention. Now they would all be playing second fiddle to an infant.

Even though Darla was not sure how she would respond to a pregnancy later in life, she loved babies. When Teddy arrived, she was the apple of Darla's eye. Anything Teddy needed or wanted took precedence over anything anyone else needed. Darla didn't realize what a fuss she was making over her youngest child. The girls smoldered when they were asked to tend to their youngest sister.

Before the pregnancy, Bob and Darla had had a weekly date night. They never traveled far, perhaps to a matinee and dinner. They left Bob Jr. in charge when he was old enough to command the household. Bob reminded Darla that it had been six months since their last date. They chose a Friday night and asked Bob Jr. to take charge. He had a football game, and Mark was the team's chief statistician. Danielle and Delilah would have to stay home with Teddy.

Danielle was enraged. She had planned to attend the dance after the game with a sophomore, Brian. Delilah didn't have plans, but she was not old enough to care for Teddy alone.

Danielle decided to invite Brian over to the house until the game was over, then wait to leave until Bob Jr. came home from the game. Bob and Darla approved of this plan.

The night of the parents' date arrived. Danielle had meticulously cleaned the house in preparation for Brian's arrival. Darla had instructed both of the girls in caring for Teddy. She had also made baked spaghetti for Brian and the two girls. By 5:00 p.m., everything was set. Bob Jr. and Mark were at school preparing for the game. Bob and Darla left for their date.

Brian was due to arrive at 6:00 p.m. At 6:15, Danielle was still waiting to heat up dinner. At 6:30, he still hadn't arrived. "Call him," suggested Delilah. It wasn't a bad idea, but Danielle hesitated. By 6:45, Delilah said, "I'm hungry. If he isn't here by seven, let's eat without him." Just then, Teddy started to cry. "You go get her. I'll call," said Danielle.

Delilah tried her best to address Teddy's need, but she still cried. In the meantime, Danielle reached Brian on his cell phone. He'd decided he'd rather attend the game. He would see her at the dance.

Delilah yelled, "Danielle, hurry! I don't know what to do with her!" Danielle, angry and disappointed, pounded up the stairs to the nursery. She picked up Teddy and shook her. "What the hell's wrong with you?" she roared. Suddently, Teddy stopped crying. Her neck had broken.

Danielle called her parents, who speeded home from their restaurant. They were too late. Teddy had died of Shaken Baby Syndrome. After a visit from a nurse practitioner, Bob called you to officiate at Teddy's funeral. Danielle was placed at a juvenile detention facility, where she would receive anger management training. She was permitted to attend her sister's funeral.

Scripture

John 20:19-23

When it was evening on that day, the first day of the week, and the doors of the house where the disciples had met were locked for fear of the Jews, Jesus came and stood among them and said, "Peace be with you." After he said this, he showed them his hands and his side. Then the disciples rejoiced when they saw the Lord. Jesus said to them again, "Peace be with you. As the Father has sent me, so I send you." When he had said this, he breathed on them and said to them, "Receive the Holy Spirit. If you forgive the sins of any, they are forgiven them; if you retain the sins of any, they are retained."

Sermon

Jesus had several missions to humanity, some of which he didn't even know about when he first began his ministry. He was able to perform spectacular miracles, including turning water into wine and feeding five thousand with five loaves and two fish. He preached, healed, trained the disciples, and taught great crowds of people. One of the themes of his teaching was forgiveness. When he revisited the disciples after his death and resurrection, he emphasized forgiveness again.

Forgiveness is a way of setting ourselves free by setting others free. We give of ourselves by letting others know that we are willing to release our anger and our resentment for any wrong they have done to us. Such an action costs us nothing. Indeed, it actually frees us.

It isn't always easy to do, however. It may take months, even years, to set a person free from wrongdoing. That person may have to admit doing wrong before we are able to forgive him or her, and that may also take time. Perhaps we will need a period of silence before we're able to face each other. The one who did wrong might have to spend some time locked away before the confrontation takes place.

Darla and Bob's family has sustained the loss of a six-month-old baby girl, Theodora Lillian, at the hands of their third child, Danielle. Danielle had been having a bad evening, made worse by Teddy's demands. In a tragic moment of rage, Danielle shook the baby violently. Teddy died as a result of her injuries.

Danielle has spent the last few days in a juvenile detention hall. She has already admitted her wrong to her parents. They have tearfully accepted her confession and have offered their forgiveness.

Tonight Danielle goes back to the facility, where she will complete her course of study. After that, she will receive counseling as she faces the more difficult task of getting used to life back at home and at school.

From all of you here, I ask for your prayers as this family mourns the loss of their youngest, but also as they seek to regain wholeness. Forgiveness is a major step toward wellness, but complete healing may take some time. God may choose to speak through any of us to give this family comfort and ease. I pray that we will heed God's call.

Prayer

Gracious God,
we thank you for the love and care in this place.
We ask that we may be generous in our support
of this family in their loss and as they rebuild.
Bless Teddy richly, as she has left our midst.
Bless Danielle, as she learns about herself and others. Amen.

Graveside Prayer

Loving God,
renew us with your love and care.
Build our strength for the days and months ahead.
Refine the gold in our character, we pray. Amen.

CHAPTER TWO

CHILDREN

CHILD DROWNS

Context

Cliff, eight, and his brother, Tyler, ten, loved the Gulf Coast of Florida. Each year, their parents packed the minivan full of water sports equipment and drove to their grandparents' bungalow on a private beach.

While on vacation, the family watched no television. They wanted their vacation to be as primitive as possible. They didn't know that even as they unloaded their gear, a hurricane was developing south of the Gulf near the Mexican coast.

Cliff was swimming when a storm began to churn the sea. Tyler was watching him from the shore, and he called his brother to swim back to safety. Cliff tried to swim back, but he was prevented by a tide, which carried him further out. Frantic, Tyler seized a rowboat and paddled out to save Cliff.

Their father Joe saw his two sons struggling in the water, and he summoned the Coast Guard, which dispatched a rescue boat. By the time it arrived, Tyler was clinging to the overturned rowboat, and Cliff was flailing a furlong away. The rescuers were able to save Tyler, but Cliff lost consciousness and disappeared from sight. Despite repeated efforts to dive down and search for him,

Cliff drowned. The rescue boat returned to shore with Tyler. Cliff's body was recovered within two days.

Scripture

Mark 4:35-41

On that day, when evening had come, he said to them, "Let us go across to the other side." And leaving the crowd behind, they took him with them in the boat, just as he was. Other boats were with him. A great windstorm arose, and the waves beat into the boat, so that the boat was already being swamped. But he was in the stern, asleep on the cushion; and they woke him up and said to him, "Teacher, do you not care that we are perishing?" He woke up and rebuked the wind, and said to the sea, "Peace! Be still!" Then the wind ceased, and there was a dead calm. He said to them, "Why are you afraid? Have you still no faith?" And they were filled with great awe and said to one another, "Who then is this, that even the wind and the sea obey him?"

Sermon

Jesus knows how powerful the sea can be. Its waves and its wind have terrified many an experienced sailor. In this story from the Gospel of Mark, the disciples demanded the help of Jesus. He responded by rebuking the wind and calming the sea. Then he questioned the disciples about their faith. The disciples, amazed at Jesus' power, responded with awe.

Cliff was a strong swimmer and a water sports enthusiast. By the summer after second grade, he was already in training as a lifeguard, following in the footsteps of his brother Tyler. He was a natural athlete, well muscled and healthy. And he was fearless, as an eight-year-old boy is fearless. Up to the point of his death, he had mastered every body of water he had ever encountered.

This happened innocently. It was Cliff's first day of vacation at his grandparents' summer home, and he had gone out for a swim. Neither he nor his parents nor his older brother knew that a hurricane was about to arrive. They were blindsided by this harsh reality.

Neither the disciples nor Jesus knew that they were about to encounter a storm at sea. They were hoping to enjoy some rest by leaving the crowd and heading toward the other side. They were already on their journey when the wind whisked around them and the water tossed their boat like a bathtub toy. The disciples were terrified.

Jesus was lying asleep, oblivious to the storm. Evidently, he had worked hard enough that day teaching and healing the people of God that much of his power had drained from him. He proved that he still had some left, however, when the disciples roused him with a sharp question, "Teacher, do you not care that we are perishing?" Then Jesus spoke a few words, and calmed the storm.

Just as Cliff struggled to swim back to shore in the midst of a hurricane, so we find ourselves in the midst of a storm of tears, of disbelief, of despair. We would do anything to regain the calm that we knew before we experienced this painful loss. Emotionally, we are out in a rowboat in the Gulf of Mexico, swirling in a maelstrom.

Our master and our friend, Jesus the Christ, is sleeping on a cushion on the stern of our boat. He will awaken to our cries for help. He will rise when he hears our anger. He will speak a few words to the storm in which we find ourselves, and it will cease. And no matter how many times we call on his name, he will calm the storm and give us his peace.

For Cliff's family, we offer our deep empathy. We may never experience the profound grief they feel, but we can wrap our arms around them, and, like Jesus, give them our peace. This doesn't take many words, but it requires much power, and much willingness to share ourselves. May we, like Jesus, rise from our sleep and calm the storm.

Prayer

Almighty God,
you move us to empathy for Cliff's family.
You provide for us your powerful Word.
You give us grace for today and hope for tomorrow.
Bless us as we mourn our loss. Amen.

Graveside Prayer

Gracious God,
you are all wisdom, power, and love.
Guide us our whole lives
with the example of your son Jesus,
so that living or dying
we may find bounteous power in him. Amen.

Child Dies of Serious Illness

Context

Jared, ten, was a blue-eyed, red-haired member of your congregation. He was bright, articulate, and had a passion for building model cars. Whenever he would finish one, he'd bring it to church and gingerly place it in your hands, as if to ask your blessing. You would marvel at it, examining it carefully, and tell him it was his best yet. He would take it back, beaming, and go home to add it to his growing collection.

His parents, Pamela and Jeremy, had supported him through a bout with cancer of the esophagus when Jared was three-and-a-half years old. Jared barely remembered the chemotherapy treatments, the hospital stays, and the trips to the emergency room. He did remember going to the Ford Museum in Dearborn, Michigan, to celebrate the five-year anniversary of his return to health.

Jared had a recurrence of this cancer when he was nine-and-a-half years old. This time, the treatment was more aggressive. The side effects were severe, including high fevers and splotchy rashes. One night, Jared had a fever and his parents rushed him to the emergency room. Pamela called you and the prayer chain. By the time you arrived at the hospital, Jared had been admitted to the Pediatric Intensive Care Unit. He was covered with a rash. He'd contracted a septic infection through the port that administered his chemotherapy. You watched as Pamela and Jeremy sat on either side of their son, alternately speaking reassurances and pressing toy cars into his hands.

Jared's hospitalization lasted three weeks. His parents were exhausted. To make matters worse, the expenses of the hospital stay had exceeded their family's insurance limit by several thousand dollars. Your church hosted three spaghetti suppers and a silent auction that offset most of the out-of-pocket costs. Late on a Saturday night, after his parents had left, Jared coded and could not be revived. Pamela called to ask you to preach at Jared's memorial service.

Scripture

Luke 2:41-51

Now every year his parents went to Jerusalem for the festival of the Passover. And when he was twelve years old, they went up as usual for the festival. When the festival was ended and they started to return, the boy Jesus stayed behind in Jerusalem, but his parents did not know it. Assuming that he was in the group of travelers, they went a day's journey. Then they started to look for him among their relatives and friends. When they did not find him, they returned to Jerusalem to search for him. After three days they found him in the temple, sitting among the teachers, listening to them and asking them questions. And all who heard him were amazed at his understanding and his answers. When his parents saw him they were astonished; and his mother said to him, "Child, why have you treated us like this? Look, your father and I have been searching for you in great anxiety." He said to them, "Why were you searching for me? Did you not know that I must be in my Father's house?" But they did not understand what he said to them. Then he went down with them and came to Nazareth, and was obedient to them. His mother treasured all these things in her heart.

Sermon

The Gospels hold only one account of our Lord Jesus Christ as a boy. It is a story of a time Jesus caused his parents great heartache. While on his family's annual trip to Jerusalem, he stayed behind to talk to the teachers at the temple. Mary and Joseph couldn't find him, even when they retraced their steps, even when they asked all of the relatives if they had seen their son. When they did find him three days later, Mary asked him a pointed question, which Jesus answered with another two questions. "Why were you searching for me? Did you not know that I must be in my Father's house?"

Life with Jesus must have been unusual. He was Joseph's son, and he would learn Joseph's trade, carpentry. He was conceived of the Holy Spirit, born to Mary, and was growing into his role as Son of God. He may have sung psalms louder than most children. He may have had a passion for helping people. He might have been an exceptionally good listener. We know that he knew the scriptures well enough to discuss them with the teachers.

Now Jared was just such an exceptional child. As a preschooler, he would run to the front of the church when it came time for the children's moment. He'd plant himself at my feet, listen intently to my question, then shout out, "God!" or if that wasn't the answer, "Jesus!" or if that wasn't right, "Church!" He knew from experience that one of those three words would answer my question.

When he first began assembling model cars, he brought one for the children's moment one Sunday. It was a 1954 Oldsmobile that he had painted a lustrous red. As he proudly displayed his handiwork, I asked him why he liked cars. He said, "Because they take us places." I wondered aloud how cars take us places, and he launched into an elaborate explanation of the internal combustion engine, which delighted all of us. So then I asked, what happens if something doesn't work. He stopped the discussion cold. "You *fix* it," he said.

Jared had his share of being fixed. His fuel line had some corrosion, which needed to be sanded off. Chemotherapy worked for his first experience with cancer of the esophagus. His recurrence was more severe. The treatment was no match for his illness. Jared succumbed to its side effects.

Like Jesus' parents, I'm sure Pamela and Jeremy were full of questions they never got to ask. They hungered for answers that never came. They sat by Jared's bed until the visiting hours were over every night, holding onto hope that became strained, then broke, leaving them awash in their tears.

Mary asked Jesus a question when she found him among the teachers at the temple. "Child, why have you treated us like this?" At the same time she asked the boy Jesus, she was asking God. Why have you treated us like this? Didn't we pray hard enough? Didn't we live right? Didn't we put all our trust in you?

When I wanted to see a master at work, I'd go watch Jared put together a car. For his first few cars, Jeremy would help him by reading him the directions, finding the pieces, and gluing parts together. When he became more proficient, Jared didn't rely on the directions solely. He had enough experience to assemble a car without following the directions word for word. He would know intuitively which part to find, which parts needed painting before gluing, how things fit together. "It's simple," he said. "If you want to know how it's going to turn out, you just look at the design and work toward it." And that's the simplest definition of vision that I know. Model cars are more predictable than life on this earth, but when we know that God has a design, we can work toward it.

Jared's parents have donated a selection of Jared's finished model cars, along with his last one, which is unfinished, to the church as a temporary display. This will serve as a memory of a boy with a vision, hands with a purpose, and a heart for the Lord.

Prayer

Loving God,
you inspire us with the lives of those we love.
You show us your strength through them.
We thank you for Jared's life among us.
We honor his memory with the words we speak of him.
We ask that you might console us in our grief.
Wrap your arms around us, we pray.
Amen.

Graveside Prayer

Gracious God,
you have put us together when we have fallen apart.
You have helped us through marriage, and childbirth,

and many a family crisis.
You are wonderfully strong and loving.
Now we ask for your help again,
to soothe our hurt
to dry our tears
to restore our wholeness.
May your name be blessed by all you have helped.
Amen.

CHILD DIES IN ACCIDENT

Context

Zachary, nine, was playing cops and robbers with his friend Billy, also nine, at Billy's house. Sarah, Billy's mother, had stepped outside to hang up some laundry. She was almost finished when she heard an explosion from within her home. As she arrived at the back door, Billy burst outside.

"I didn't mean to! I didn't mean to!" he sputtered.

Sarah caught him and knelt in front of him, holding his shoulders. "What, son?"

"I didn't mean to shoot the gun!"

Sarah raced to the bedroom, where she and her husband Larry kept a loaded handgun in their nightstand for security. On the floor, Zachary lay lifeless, with a single wound in his heart. Sarah composed herself, and then called 911. She called Larry to come home, and then she called a neighbor to stay with Billy.

Zachary's mother Joyce met Sarah, who had ridden the ambulance with Zachary, at Children's Hospital. The boy was pronounced dead on arrival. Joyce refused all comfort offered by Sarah, vowing to pursue revenge through the court system. In the meantime, Larry arrived home to find that Billy had run away.

Joyce called to ask you to do the funeral, but she requested that Billy's family be prevented from attending. Later that day, Billy was arrested and taken to a juvenile detention facility in a distant city to await trial. Sarah and Larry put their house on the market and left town to be near their son.

Scripture

Genesis 4:8-16

Cain said to his brother Abel, "Let us go out to the field." And when they were in the field, Cain rose up against his brother Abel, and killed him. Then the LORD said to Cain, "Where is your brother Abel?" He said, "I do not know; am I my brother's keeper?" And the LORD said, "What have you done? Listen; your brother's blood is crying out to me from the ground! And now you are cursed from the ground, which has opened its mouth to receive your brother's blood from your hand. When you till the ground, it will no longer yield to you its strength; you will be a fugitive and a wanderer on the earth." Cain said to the LORD, "My punishment is greater than I can bear! Today you have driven me away from the soil, and I shall be hidden from your face; I shall be a fugitive and a wanderer on the earth, and anyone who meets me may kill me." Then the LORD said to him, "Not so! Whoever kills Cain will suffer a sevenfold vengeance." And the LORD put a mark on Cain, so that no one who came upon him would kill him. Then Cain went away from the presence of the LORD, and settled in the land of Nod, east of Eden.

Sermon

Adam and Eve had eaten forbidden fruit of the tree of knowledge, and now they knew good from evil. Eve, with the Lord's help, produced a son, Cain, the first child born to human parents. It would seem that all was right with the world.

Abel was the second son of Adam and Eve. Once the two sons had matured, they found they had one of the oldest natural enmities—Cain was a farmer, and Abel was a herdsman. When it came time for the two men to give their offerings, God approved Abel's sacrifice, but did not approve Cain's. This sent Cain into a rage, and he killed Abel in revenge.

God did not kill Cain. He dealt with his denial. He listened to his despair. He didn't mitigate his punishment. Finally, he protected Cain by putting a mark on him.

Curiously, we do not hear about Abel after he died. We don't know whether or not he received a burial. We don't know how Adam and Eve felt about losing one son by the other's hand. We don't know how they lived with their sorrow. We do know that they had another son, Seth. That tells us that eventually, their lives moved on.

Our situation is different today. During a game, one boy died, and the other ran away. Between cops and robbers, there is a natural enmity. The boys were competing. They were in the heat of a critical moment when Billy took his parents' handgun out of hiding and pointed it at Zachary. He didn't know it was loaded. He didn't know how to shoot. He had helped himself to disaster.

Zachary received the consequences of Billy's action, just as Abel received Cain's unbridled anger. He became the victim in a game that had gone too far. Now he's gone.

However the courts deal with Billy will depend on human-made laws. Billy will still have God's offer of salvation through Jesus Christ, which Zachary has now received. God will have his mark on Billy, so that no one may harm him. God has accepted Zachary into God's kingdom, which is the pearl of great price, the mustard seed that grows into a bush, the lost coin that is found again. No one can ever harm Zachary again, and God has wiped away his every tear.

Here on earth, we are in spiritual warfare. We witness violence; we feel sorrow; we want revenge. God may wonder why we can't all just get along. If loving our neighbor was that easy, God might have given that commandment to some of the lesser creatures. Instead he gave it to us, for we are a little lower than the angels.

Prayer

Almighty God,
we are crestfallen at our loss.
We look to you for comfort and peace.

May we look to you for salvation.
May we look to each other for help.
May we learn to love our neighbor as ourselves. Amen.

Graveside Prayer

Gracious God,
your steadfast love never fails.
Help us to journey into your heart,
so that in this life, we may see your goodness
in the people we seek to help.
Guide us in our efforts to love one another. Amen.

Child Dies Due to Mistreatment

Context

Timmy, three, was the youngest of five children born to one mother and three fathers. His half-brothers and half-sister had little supervision at home and no respect for themselves or others. They teased and harassed him. He was too fearful to retaliate, and he had no friends to defend him, except for his grandmother, who lived across the street.

One late afternoon, when the rest of the children had come home from school, their mother went out for a few drinks after work. Timmy, hungry, entered the kitchen, where his half-sister was trying to prepare dinner. He whined. She told him to go away. He trotted into the family room, where his half-brothers were watching television. He stood in front of the screen and announced that he was hungry. They responded by pushing him around until he fell against the coffee table, blackening both of his eyes. They carried him, screaming, to a hallway closet, and shoved him inside, breaking one of his arms. Then they locked the door.

Three hours later, their mother came home drunk. When she asked where Timmy was, he yelled from inside the closet. She opened the door and he fell out on the floor, whimpering. By this time, his eyes had swollen shut and the broken bone protruded through his skin.

"Who did this to him?" asked his mother, eying the older boys.

"He did it to himself!" said one of them.

"Get up, Timmy!" she snarled.

Timmy rose with difficulty. His face turned to the sound of his mother's voice.

Crack! She slapped the side of his face. In terrible pain, he turned to run out the door, cradling his broken arm with his other hand. Once outside, he dashed blindly across the street to his grandmother's house, directly into the path of a neighbor's SUV. He sustained fatal injuries from the impact.

You were visiting Timmy's grandmother, a parishioner. You witnessed this accident from her front window and called an ambulance. You then rushed to the street to see how you could help. Timmy died in your arms. His grandmother asked you to officiate at Timmy's funeral service. His mother was charged with child neglect and abuse. The driver was charged with vehicular manslaughter.

Scripture

Luke 23:44-49

It was now about noon, and darkness came over the whole land until three in the afternoon, while the sun's light failed; and the curtain of the temple was torn in two. Then Jesus, crying with a loud voice, said, "Father, into your hands I commend my spirit." Having said this, he breathed his last. When the centurion saw what had taken place, he praised God and said, "Certainly this man was innocent." And when all the crowds who had gathered there for the spectacle saw what had taken place, they returned home, beating their breasts. But all his acquaintances, including the women who had followed him from Galilee, stood at a distance, watching these things.

Sermon

Jesus, an innocent man, died a horrible death. Out of reach of the ones he loved, he was powerless to save himself. In Luke's account of his death, Jesus' last words were part of a child's prayer, "Father, into your hands I commend my spirit." Many of those who witnessed his death despised him. After seeing him die, some of them felt great remorse.

Timmy's grandmother remembers him as a loving child, committed to righting the wrongs of the household in which he lived. He did not ask for exceptional things. He desired the attention of his mother, regular meals, and respect from his siblings. In return, he received a broken arm and two blackened eyes, injuries that sent him screaming to his grandmother and led to his death by manslaughter.

As in the death of our Lord, we know that there are those who watched Timmy die who knew he was innocent, undeserving of the cruelty of those who had punished him. These persons knew that Timmy was trying to return to one from whom he had received comfort and affirmation. They saw him run to her blindly, without caution. They watched from afar, powerless to warn him of an oncoming vehicle.

Timmy's death, like Christ's, will not be in vain. His neighbors have set up a watch system that will prevent such injuries from happening again. Timmy's mother and the driver of the vehicle have been charged and are expected to serve maximum sentences. The city police have doubled their forces in the neighborhood. The human structures are in place.

So are the divine structures. God has promised us help in this life and a home in the life to come. Today, Timmy lives in paradise. He has regular meals. He is given good attention. He is respected. He is receiving everything he lacked on earth, everything denied him, everything he missed as a member of his household. Now he is a member of the household of God, where he is loved.

Whether or not we are part of Timmy's neighborhood, we are sobered by this tragedy. Now we are on alert for recklessness, neglect, and abuse. We know that Jesus' command to love one another is a responsibility and a privilege. May we go forward from this place boldly, with love for God and neighbor.

Prayer

Gracious God,
we offer thanksgiving for Timmy's life,
for the love he showed,
for the hope he embodied.
May his courage live on in us.
May the love of Christ inspire our care of each other. Amen.

Graveside Prayer

Gracious God,
may we go from this place empowered
to love as you have loved,
energetically, selflessly, and with compassion.
Comfort us in our loss,
and give us your peace. Amen.

CHAPTER THREE

YOUTH AND YOUNG ADULTS

YOUTH DIES AS DRIVER IN CAR ACCIDENT

Context

Steven, eighteen, was the valedictorian of his high school class. He lived in a suburban development in one of the larger cities in the United States. During the summer before his freshman year of college, he worked for a group of student painters, a job he hoped to keep through his university career. His employer liked him because he was reliable. He never called in sick or hung over. He was always on time to drive to his next assignment.

One day, the assistant manager was attending a funeral. The manager assigned Steven to drive the rickety truck to the group's first assignment of the day, a historic schoolhouse in a rural area fifty miles away. The rest of the students piled into the truck, and Steven took the wheel.

They were only a few blocks away from their home office when Steven tried the brakes—they did not work. He cried to Roy, who was sitting in the front passenger seat, "What should I do!" "Find a curb to rub against," Roy responded, "and lay on the horn!"

Steven honked his way through two intersections, and convinced his friends to jump out. At the third intersection, the driver of a delivery truck was unable to stop. He clipped the driver's side of the painters' truck, killing Steven instantly. The other students sustained only minor injuries.

Steven and his parents were your parishioners. His parents called from the hospital to ask you to officiate at his funeral.

Scripture

Matthew 16:24-26

Then Jesus told his disciples, "If any want to become my followers, let them deny themselves and take up their cross and follow me. For those who want to save their life will lose it, and those who lose their life for my sake will find it. For what will it profit them if they gain the whole world but forfeit their life? Or what will they give in return for their life?"

Sermon

Jesus sometimes had to be stern with his disciples. This scripture passage follows Jesus' rebuke of Peter, after Peter had refused to believe that Jesus would die at the hands of the elders and the chief priests, then ascend to heaven. After this rebuke, Jesus turned to the disciples and gave them this hard word. None of the Gospel accounts tell us if the disciples confirmed or denied what Jesus said.

When Steven's manager asked him to drive the pickup truck, he didn't question authority. He was like the rest of the disciples who neither accepted nor contradicted Jesus' teaching on the sacrifices one must make as a disciple. He knew that he had to accept his manager's authority to be able to retain his job as a student painter for the summers to come. He didn't know, however, what kind of shape the truck was in. That was Steven's cross to bear, and he shouldered it in obedience.

Steven had always been an outstanding student and a leader in the youth group at church. It was Steven who presented the idea of a youth mission trip to the administrative council of the church. The youth had long desired to go on such a trip together, but never had the gumption to approach the administrative council for a source of funding. The council wasn't able to fund the mission trip, but it suggested several fund-raisers and volunteered some of its leadership to shepherd the projects. Steven's proposal proved to be the catalyst for a youth mission program at our church. He was able to lead in obedience to greater authority.

I chaperoned one of those mission trips. It was Steven's second year at the mission, and he was very much in evidence, directing the efforts of the younger children, asking the adult leadership what to do next after a project was completed, and seizing the hose during the daily water fights. Of course, he would always help arrange a truce when an adult announced that supper was ready.

Steven did love his life, and he was looking forward to a bright future, attending his university on a full scholarship, choosing a major, perhaps someday leading a corporation. But driving that pickup truck through those three intersections, he had the safety of the other passengers in mind. He asked Roy how to stop the truck, then failing that, he told him to tell the others to jump off. The third intersection was fatal for him, but the others were safe. Protecting the others, and losing his own life, he gained a place in heaven.

Those of us who are left here on earth have the difficulty. We need to continue with our lives without Steven. Knowing that he is enjoying his life in heaven even more than he enjoyed life on earth is of some consolation. Knowing that he saved the lives of others is also a solace. As we imagine him with his Lord, let us also remember that we have a place in heaven, and hope to meet him again by and by.

Prayer

Great God,
 we praise you for Steven, this fine young man
 who took up his cross and valued others' lives

more than his own.
May we heed his example
and show greater love. Amen.

Graveside Prayer

Gracious God,
you give us wonderful people to love.
Help us all our lives through to appreciate those
who have laid down their lives for their friends.
Bless us as we live this life joyfully,
and anticipate the life to come. Amen.

YOUTH DIES AS PASSENGER IN CAR ACCIDENT

Context

Jacqui, fifteen, loved to date older boys. When her boyfriends were old enough to drive, her parents insisted that each have a 3.0 grade average and come from an upright family. These limits didn't stop Jacqui. She always had a retinue of beaus.

When Randall, the captain of the wrestling team, asked Jacqui to the Junior-Senior Prom, she was elated. Jacqui's mother agreed to make her a dress. Her two older sisters helped her choose the pattern and fabric and promised to share some of their makeup.

On the night of the dance, Jacqui was resplendent. Her father took pictures of her coming down the stairs, posing in the doorway, and illuminated by the dining room chandelier. He snapped a few more when Randall arrived. The couple left after the obligatory safety lecture, eager to begin their evening together.

Jacqui and Randall danced almost every dance. When they weren't dancing, Randall disappeared, ostensibly to go to the bathroom. When he came back, he smelled of alcohol, but his dancing improved, so Jacqui didn't mind.

Toward the end of the dance, another couple invited both of them to an after-prom party. Jacqui said yes, but said she would have to phone home first. She called to ask her father's permission, which he denied. Jacqui asked Randall to take her home.

Knowing that Randall had been drinking, Brent and Talia offered to take Jacqui home, but Randall insisted on driving Jacqui home himself. It had rained and was still drizzling. The road to Jacqui's home was as slick and curvy as an anaconda. Randall hit a curb and the car flipped over. Jacqui died instantly. Randall woke up in a hospital room with a concussion and several broken bones. He was charged with vehicular manslaughter and failure to control his vehicle.

When Jacqui's friends heard that she had died, they refrigerated their corsages to preserve them for her funeral. They would lay them on her casket in remembrance.

Scripture

John 6:35-40

Jesus said to them, "I am the bread of life. Whoever comes to me will never be hungry, and whoever believes in me will never be thirsty. But I said to you that you have seen me and yet do not believe. Everything that the Father gives me will come to me, and anyone who comes to me I will never drive away; for I have come down from heaven, not to do my own will, but the will of him who sent me. And this is the will of him who sent me, that I should lose nothing of all that he has given me, but raise it up on the last day. This is indeed the will of my Father, that all who see the Son and believe in him may have eternal life; and I will raise them up on the last day."

Sermon

Jesus was speaking to a crowd of people who had followed him to the far side of the sea. They wanted to see him feed the five thousand again. They wanted manna to rain down from heaven, as it had in Moses's time. They were hungry. They wanted Jesus to fill them.

Jesus responded that he is the bread of life, that their needs could be fulfilled in him. This was a relief to some people who understood his metaphor, but a puzzle to others. Jesus was foretelling the sacrifice of his body and the sacrament that would commemorate his death. The Jews questioned Jesus and argued among themselves. Even the disciples said, "This teaching is difficult; who can accept it?"

Jacqui struggled to believe that Jesus had died for her and that he would fulfill her needs. Her Sunday school teacher knew that, just like the disciples, she was having difficulty. Jacqui asked her teacher after class one Sunday, "Does this mean that Jesus is all we will need?" Her teacher explained that we need to look to Jesus as we might consult a mentor or a friend. She said we must learn about Jesus and take his example and his preaching together, that they are trustworthy.

Jacqui was still hungering and thirsting for righteousness after this conversation. She was like the crowd that had followed Jesus to the far side of the sea. In her life, there was still something missing. She searched for wholeness by dating several upperclassmen. These young men were older and Jacqui saw them as wiser, providing assurance, while she sought to complete herself.

She will be remembered as the freshman who got asked to the Junior-Senior Prom, a fun-loving girl with a fine spirit. Members of her family, who supported her and who protected her so well, have told me that they are grateful for the time they have had with her, and that they are hopeful that others at her school will learn from her life, not only the disaster of her death, but the beauty of her days and the joy of her life to come.

When Jesus discovered that his friend Lazarus had died, he wept; and so we weep today. Jesus wept, but he also said to his disciples, "So you have pain now; but I will see you again, and your hearts will rejoice, and no one will take your joy from you" (John 16:22). Christ will strengthen us, in the bread and the cup of the sacrament, in his prayer for us, in the embrace of friends and neighbors. He will not leave us orphaned, but he will be with us until the end of the age.

Prayer

Loving God,
we are grateful for Jacqui's life
for her beauty and lovingkindness,
for her searching and spirituality.
We ask that, now that you have received her,
she may feel complete as never before,
consoled by your abiding love. Amen.

Graveside Prayer

Gracious God,
you give us a life lived to your glory,
a life to admire—Jacqui's life.
We struggle to be content with our memories.
We hurt more than we know.
Bring us to Jesus for consolation,
for truly, he is our all in all. Amen.

Youth Dies of Serious Illness

Context

Barry, thirteen, developed leukemia when he was three years old. He survived three times, each time entering the hospital for chemotherapy. The treatments had made him sick enough not to attend school for a few weeks each time, so he'd had tutors, sometimes for more than half of the school year. His studies progressed on schedule, and he had been able to graduate from elementary school. During the end-of-the-year ceremony, he wore his mortarboard proudly, his bald head shining underneath his cap.

During the first semester of his seventh-grade year, just when Barry's hair had grown back, just when his parents had paid off his last hospitalization, Sharon, Barry's oncologist, called his mother while she was at work. "Are you sitting down?" she asked.

Jane sat. "What is it?" she asked.

Sharon intoned, "It's back already."

Jane expressed the depth of her disappointment in a single word: "No!"

Jane took Barry to his oncologist the next day for further tests. The tests confirmed Sharon's diagnosis. Barry asked Sharon about his choices.

"You do have a couple," she said. She told him about an experimental chemotherapy that might work quickly, but would have severe side effects. Or, she said, he could do nothing. "If you do nothing, you will die. If you try the experimental drug, you might still die, but you will have tried the drug for someone else who might benefit from it."

Barry opted to try the experimental drug. Jane wanted to know if there were any other options. Sharon said that Barry's leukemia had resisted all conventional therapies. Experimental drugs had proved beneficial in other patients.

"Besides, Mom," said Barry, "Trying this will help other people if it doesn't help me."

Jane relented. She quit her job so that she could spend more time with her son. Barry's father, Doug, obtained permission to cut his work hours to half time for the same rate of pay.

The side effects of the experimental drug were so brutal that Barry spent two nights in the emergency room. Both times, however, he was released to go home. This was a relief to Jane and Doug, who wanted to spend every moment with their son.

At Christmastime, Barry's tutors formed a choir and went caroling together in his neighborhood. They stopped at his door and sang their full repertoire. Barry lumbered to the door during the first carol, leaning on his father for support. Jane gave the carolers cookies, and they yelled, "Merry Christmas!" Barry tried to yell back, but he was unable to speak the words. Once the door had closed, he said, "That was nice," then fell asleep on the couch for the rest of the evening.

Sharon called Jane to invite her and Barry to her office. She told them, "I have good news, and I have bad news. First, the good news—the experimental chemotherapy shows every sign of working. Now, the bad news—it is working on every kind of leukemia but yours." She thanked Barry for being brave enough to withstand a trial of this drug, and asked him if he wanted to continue. Weak and hardly able to speak, he said no. Sharon told Jane to take him home and love him.

In the coming weeks, Barry had a slight rally. Christmas came and went, marked by the traditional exchange of gifts, the Christmas Eve service, and the Christmas breakfast of French toast with strawberry syrup. After Christmas, Barry's health declined. He agreed to hospice care, and a hospital bed was delivered and placed in the living room of his home.

Barry died peacefully and painlessly with his parents and a hospice nurse's aide at his side, but not before he'd spoken his wish to give his entire hat collection, and it was vast, to another young cancer patient. Jane called you to ask you to perform a memorial service. The tutor choir volunteered to sing a few hymns.

Scripture

Matthew 16:21-23

From this time on, Jesus began to show his disciples that he must go to Jerusalem and undergo great suffering at the hands of the elders and chief priests and scribes, and be killed, and on the third day be raised. And Peter took him aside and began to rebuke him, saying, "God forbid it, Lord! This must never happen to you." But he turned and said to Peter, "Get behind me, Satan! You are a stumbling block to me; for you are setting your mind not on divine things but on human things."

Sermon

Peter was the leader among the disciples, always ready to try something new, always outspoken, even to the point of contradicting Jesus. In this scripture passage, he does just that, offending

Jesus and causing him to correct Peter pointedly. Peter has just received the keys to the kingdom of heaven, and he takes Jesus' rebuke seriously enough that he doesn't respond.

Jesus rebukes Peter for setting his mind on human things rather than on divine things. While we are living, this is an easy mistake for us to make. We get involved in grocery shopping, golf outings, volunteer opportunities—all of the day-to-day things that keep our lives busy and productive. We fail to notice that there are other people struggling nobly with their lives, making serious decisions, even helping others out despite their depleted physical condition.

Barry began fighting leukemia when he was three years old. At that time, he received much family support, and he was able to feel better soon after his chemotherapy ended. When he had a relapse in third grade, five other children in his class, including one girl, decided to shave their heads in sympathy. They all showed up in his hospital room one Saturday morning, along with the barber who did the honors. At Christmastime, the tutor choir went to visit Barry. Today they are singing at his funeral.

Arranged around the room, you will find Barry's forty-two hats, all of which he has donated to another child undergoing chemotherapy. He wanted them to go to someone who would use them. He told his mother he didn't want her to make his room a museum, with the hats as a primary display.

The height of Barry's altruism was his willingness to try an experimental chemotherapy for leukemia. While he hoped that it would work for him on his disease, he knew that if it didn't work for him, it might work for someone else. Jane allowed him to try, knowing that the odds were that it would not be effective for him. She and Doug stayed close by Barry's side to help him cope with the side effects.

Jesus rebuked Peter for placing human things over divine things. Barry was one who was able to focus on the divine. He gave his beloved hats to another child. He donated his body to science. He gave his heart to the Lord. Now his spirit has gone up to heaven, and we on earth are left to marvel. Praise be to God for his son, Barry!

Prayer

Almighty God,
you give us courage for living.
Sometimes, we even find courage for dying.
In Barry, we have seen courage for others.
We praise you for this strength of his.
We ask you for your care of him,
now that he has entered your kingdom. Amen.

Graveside Prayer

Gracious God,
you give us wonderful people to love.
We praise your name, and we honor you
for giving us Barry.
Now, as we have given him back to you,
we ask you for the strength to live
powerful lives in his memory. Amen.

Youth Murdered

Context

Lynne, a seventeen-year-old girl in your community, was murdered at her home. The girl was popular. She was a majorette, a concert band member, and an officer for her class. She was killed by Larry, nineteen, who had asked her on a date. When she refused, his anger became uncontrollable. He broke into her home, stabbed her repeatedly, and left to wander the streets.

Elyssa and Darrell returned home from a movie to find their daughter lying on the living room floor, barely breathing. Darrell raced to call 911 while Elyssa, a nurse, stayed on the floor with her, checking for any sign of life. Lynne was pronounced dead on arrival at the local hospital. A chaplain and a social worker brought the news to Lynne's parents, who collapsed on each other in tears.

The police found Larry sitting on a bench in the city park, the knife still in his hand, his body shaking uncontrollably. He left with them peacefully.

When a teenager is murdered, the youthful illusion of immortality is shattered. Families wonder if their children are safe. Affirming the ongoing care of God is as important as eulogizing the young person.

Scripture

Luke 1:46-55

And Mary said,
"My soul magnifies the Lord,
and my spirit rejoices in God my Savior,
for he has looked with favor on the lowliness of his servant.
Surely, from now on all generations will call me blessed;
for the Mighty One has done great things for me,
and holy is his name.
His mercy is for those who fear him
from generation to generation.
He has shown strength with his arm;
he has scattered the proud in the thoughts of their hearts.
He has brought down the powerful from their thrones,
and lifted up the lowly;
he has filled the hungry with good things,
and sent the rich away empty.
He has helped his servant Israel,
in remembrance of his mercy,
according to the promise he made to our ancestors,
to Abraham and to his descendants forever."

Sermon

Mary was a very young woman when the angel Gabriel came to her with news of great joy. He told her that she was to be the mother of Jesus the Christ, the Son of God. At first, this came as a shock. Mary was "much perplexed." She was earthbound enough to want answers to her questions. She was also faithful enough to accept the angel's commission and rejoice at God's favor in choosing her to bear God's son.

Today, we are celebrating the life of just such a young woman. Lynne was pretty. She was lively. She had great vitality. What's more, she had musical ability, twirling ability, and a spiritual gift of leadership. She was generous with her time and attention to her friends at school, and even with people who didn't know her well. She took seriously God's command to love others as God had loved her.

Then her life ended. Lynne, God's favored one, was murdered in her home by someone who wanted a little more of her than she was able to give. As she struggled to regain control, her attacker lost control. She was the victim of a brutal act of one who had lost his grip on his own humanity. Lynne died. Her vitality ebbed away. One who will now pay a heavy price for his sin squandered her life force.

Like Mary, I'm sure Lynne questioned God while she tried to fend off this threat. She may have asked, "Why me?" or "Why now?" She may have asked God's help, or wondered why no one responded to her cries for help. Perhaps she couldn't cry out. Perhaps she realized she was overmatched. At some point, she gave up the struggle.

Now we are left with questions. Why Lynne? Why now? If God favored Lynne, why did God let this happen? People have been asking these same questions for centuries. Some have found ways to make sense of senselessness. Some have devised ways to protect themselves against evil. Some have learned to rely on God. The truth is that we are all vulnerable, and that makes us fearful and anxious.

Lynne energized those of us who knew her. We were uplifted by her vitality. She had a way of encouraging people that renewed us. We knew she could bring the best out in us. We are better people because we knew her. By her example, she taught us how to love. And love is the absence of fear.

God orders our lives. God points us toward wholeness. For those who lack resources, God provides them. For those who have more than they need, God inspires them to give. "He has brought down the powerful from their thrones, and lifted up the lowly. He has filled the hungry with good things, and sent the rich away empty." We are even blessed in our mourning, for God will comfort us. In our pain, we will find solace.

And Lynne will live on in our hearts, inspiring our love of one another, guiding us in our struggles with faith, helping us set limits in our relationships. While she was living on earth with us, we appreciated God's grace in her. Now that she has departed from us, we will honor her memory by using what she taught us.

Sometime in the next few months, we may find ourselves relaxing at the end of a hard day, enjoying a few moments of peace. We may think of Lynne, about something she said, something she did, or one of her favorite expressions. But instead of weeping, we will smile, involuntarily, grateful for the life she lived among us, and we will know that we were well loved.

Prayer

Loving God,
you are wonderfully generous and kind.
You gave us Lynne to love,
and our hearts grew large to receive her.
When she departed from us,
our hearts grew even larger to accept her death.
God, today we have stretch marks on our hearts.
We miss Lynne terribly.
Protect and guide us, we pray.
We rely on you for comfort and strength.
We pray in the name of the Good Shepherd.
Amen.

Graveside Prayer

Everlasting God,
you offer us your help for the present
and your home for the future.
Your mercy is tender.
Your protection is sure.

Guide our days, ease our nights.
Let your love be perfected in us.
We pray in the name of the one who sits at your right hand.
Amen.

YOUTH DIES ACCIDENTALLY

Context

Brandon, a sixteen-year-old teen, drowned in a hot tub in his home. Four empty beer cans were found on the side of the tub. No one else had been in the room. His mother and father found him when they returned home. His father called 911 while his mother attempted CPR. The boy was pronounced dead on arrival at the hospital.

Brandon's death became a much-publicized coroner's case. People who knew him couldn't believe that he had purposely taken his own life. He had many friends, both boys and girls, and was on good terms with all of them. He was doing exceptionally well in school. He had just been nominated for the National Honor Society.

When uncertainty surrounds the cause of death, it is important to emphasize what is certain—the constancy of God's loving care of the bereaved family and friends, who struggle to endure the pain of loss.

Scripture

Acts 20:8-10

There were many lamps in the room upstairs where we were meeting. A young man named Eutychus, who was sitting in the window, began to sink off into a deep sleep while Paul talked still longer. Overcome by sleep, he fell to the ground three floors below and was picked up dead. But Paul went down, and bending over him took him in his arms, and said, "Do not be alarmed, for his life is in him."

Sermon

The story of Eutychus is one of the few accidental deaths mentioned in the Bible. Some people died naturally at a young age. Many died tragically, including our Lord and Savior Jesus Christ, who was crucified, pilloried between two thieves, in his early thirties. In the days following Jesus' death, people would be detained and tortured for their beliefs. No one knew these deaths would happen. People in authority, people with weapons, people passionate about law and order ended many young lives with decisive forcefulness.

In the case of Eutychus, death was accidental. He was sitting in a precarious position, falling asleep. His mishap was caused by loss of equilibrium. Eutychus was revived by Paul, but we can imagine the shock and sorrow of his loved ones as they believed him forever lost to them.

The death of a young person is intolerable for us as family and friends. As teens mature, we nurture the potential we see. We encourage the pursuit of dreams. We ensure comfort. We provide for needs. Through all of this, we grow to love them. We have much invested in them. When a young life ends, for whatever reason, the loss cuts us to the heart.

As we mourn the loss of Brandon, we will try to make sense of this tragedy. Even now, the medical examiner is looking for the cause of his death. The result of his analysis will render information for our minds. Information dispels fear. But it won't ensure our comfort.

Those who have read the Bible may note that Eutychus fell three stories, but they won't know much about how he lived. We can infer that he was serious about hearing God's word. He was willing to spend an evening listening to the apostle Paul rather than engaging in the more typical pursuits of young people of his day. He wanted to learn how the love of Christ was transforming his world.

Brandon was loving and helpful to the people in his family. Anytime his older siblings needed a babysitter, he was ready to stay the night. He'd romp all over the house or the yard with his nieces and nephews until bedtime came. When the children were under his care, he would always call his brothers and sisters if he noticed the slightest symptom of illness or injury. He wanted to make sure the children got the attention they needed.

Brandon was a good student. He especially enjoyed research projects that included giving presentations. He had a way with words and a compelling presence. He could captivate a classroom with a speech against abortion or euthanasia. "Brandon was pro-life to the last," said one of his teachers.

Catechism at St. Ambrose Catholic Church was the setting for Brandon's acceptance of Christ as his Lord and Savior. He came home after one class and told his mother he wanted to be a disciple, that he was called to follow Christ. Wondering what all of this might mean, his mother asked him if he intended to pursue a religious vocation. "No," said Brandon, "because I want to have lots of children." He told her maybe he would become a deacon later on.

It is hard to believe that a young man of such vitality would die so early. It is equally hard to believe that one who valued life so highly would endanger himself. Much is yet to be discovered about the circumstances of this accidental death. Facts must be found; conclusions must be drawn. Now we see in the mirror dimly. Then we will see face-to-face.

Until the day that we meet Brandon again, we will have a yearning for him and a quest for information about him. We will not stop searching until all is revealed. But our comfort will come from God who created all of us—our families and friends who love us, and all others who encourage us. One day we will be complete, as Brandon is now complete, in heaven. Until then, we wait for answers, offering consolation to each other.

Prayer

Almighty God,
  we are grateful for the life of Brandon
  for in him we saw such potential
  and it heartened us to watch him grow in your image.

As we give him back to you,
give us the strength to live the rest of our days
with your commandments in our minds
and your consolation for our hearts.
Amen.

Graveside Prayer

Gracious God,
you give us wonderful people to love.
We learn to care for them;
we become attached to them,
for you have told us to love one another.
When we lose one whom we love,
our hearts ache,
for you made us to live in relationship with each other.
Be our guide and our comfort,
and may we find joy even in our sorrow.
Amen.

YOUTH COMPLETES SUICIDE

Context

Fifteen-year-old Kate was a quiet child. She went to school every morning, came home on time, then spent most of the evening by herself, leaving her room only for supper. The third of seven children, her lack of contribution to the family conversation was not noticed.

When the oldest, Charles Jr., left home to go to college, Kate won a family lottery to inherit his bedroom. When she moved in, she put no decoration on the walls. The room was adorned only with a faded red ribbed-cord bedspread, which she always smoothed over the bed linens.

Kate loved to listen to popular music. When she spent time alone, she listened to the sexy lyrics and driving beat, and dreamed of the special man who would someday give her all of his attention. When she turned off the music to go to bed, she would sift through her images, humming softly.

One day at school, Kate caught the fancy of a young man. He invited her to a dance, and then took a detour on the way home. He parked his car in a secluded spot and raped her.

At home, Kate's mother asked her about her date. Still in shock, Kate said, "Good." As she turned to mount the stairs to her bedroom, her mother asked, "What did you do?" Kate said, "Nothing," and continued to mount the stairs.

The next morning, when Kate's mother entered her room to wake her, she found her daughter had hanged herself using her bedspread on a rod in her clothes closet. A suicide note read, "It's not your fault."

Kate's mother shrieked. When she had composed herself, she called 911. She also called you, and asked you to officiate at Kate's memorial service.

Scripture

Acts 7:54–8:1a

When they heard these things, they became enraged and ground their teeth at Stephen. But filled with the Holy Spirit, he gazed into heaven and saw the glory of God and Jesus standing at the right hand of God. "Look," he said, "I see the heavens opened and the Son of Man standing at the right hand of God!" But they covered their ears, and with a loud shout all rushed together against him. Then they dragged him out of the city and began to stone him; and the witnesses laid their coats at the feet of a young man named Saul. While they were stoning Stephen, he prayed, "Lord Jesus, receive my spirit." Then he knelt down and cried out in a loud voice, "Lord, do not hold this sin against them." When he had said this, he died. And Saul approved of their killing him.

Sermon

Stephen was one of the early Christian martyrs, later canonized as a saint. He believed so strongly in the message of salvation brought by Jesus Christ that he caught a glimpse of heaven while his persecutors glowered. So consumed with anger were they that they pursued Stephen and subjected him to a most cruel death. As they stoned him, Stephen forgave them.

As far as we know, Kate did not have a hoard of people who pursued her. She had only a wistful longing for someone to love her. Her favorite Christmas gift was an album of popular romantic songs by a contemporary artist. Her favorite pastime was listening to this recording or the radio, and imagining life as one beloved by another.

Courtship and marriage are not lofty dreams. Most people marry at least once, and almost everyone has had a sweetheart or two. It is normal for teenagers to have crushes, fall in love, and break up after a spat. Kate had her share of male friends but her date for the dance was her first since entering high school. It proved to be her last.

Even though her mother asked her about the date, Kate refused to disclose what had so troubled her. It was not unusual for Kate to be circumspect, so her mother asked no more questions. Whatever happened had upset Kate enough that she chose to end her life. But before she acted on that choice, she took the time to write a simple note, "It's not your fault."

Jesus was a great liberator of people. He freed people from their illnesses and injuries. He freed people from evil spirits. He freed people from relationships that prevented them from doing God's will. He freed them from idolatry. Following in his footsteps, Kate freed her family from guilt.

We don't know what went through Kate's mind in her final moments. We don't know what pain she had endured. We do know that the pain was so great that she felt she had to kill herself to be rid of it. She made a forever decision in a moment in which agony seemed to be hurtling toward her like the stones that killed Stephen.

What is left for us—Kate's family and friends? Of course, we have memories. We will remember the sound of her voice as she sang along to her favorite songs. We will remember the look on her face when she announced that she was going to her first high school dance. We will remember the dress she chose. But ultimately, we will remember the forgiveness she granted us when she wrote, "It's not your fault."

And like Stephen, we have a vision of our salvation. It is the glory of God and Jesus standing at his right hand. It is the power of the Holy Spirit who completes our prayers. It is the hope of seeing Kate again, radiant and whole.

Prayer

Almighty God,
we are grateful for the life of Kate.
We are grateful for the life of Stephen
We are grateful for the life of Jesus Christ.
All of them freely offered us release from guilt.
All of them await us in heaven. Amen.

Graveside Prayer

Gracious God,
you give us the power to heal,
the power to begin anew,
the power to hope afresh.
Abide with us all through our lives
and strengthen our hearts,
that we may be strong for others. Amen.

Youth Dies as Victim of School Violence

Context

Tuesday began as a typical day at the junior high school, except that more students than usual had called in sick. Several of the students and a few of the teachers had shared a virus. Beatrice, the school secretary, logged the excused absences and handed the list to Karen, the principal.

"Lot of that flu," Beatrice commented.

"Yes, that'll happen around this time of year. Have you gotten your shot?" asked Karen.

"Yes, last week. How 'bout you?"

Karen was still trying to find the time. She had two children at home sick, and her husband couldn't afford to take another day off. She would have to take her shift tomorrow. She filed the list and left the office to make her morning rounds.

At the opposite end of the hall, a young man dressed in jeans and a parka entered the building. Karen immediately recognized him as Jake, a boy who had failed a grade before finally graduating. He had been in and out of trouble constantly. Karen had often disciplined him.

"Jake, what are you doing here?" asked Karen as she approached the boy.

"I came to see you," he said, drawing a handgun from his pocket and pointing it shakily at the principal.

Karen was speechless. She'd been trained to respond to this kind of crisis, but she instantly forgot what to say. She remembered only to remain calm.

Then David walked into the hallway from the boys' restroom. He'd had a touch of the flu, too, and was walking toward the office when he noticed Jake and the gun. Incensed, he shouted, "Hey! You can't shoot the principal! She's good to us!"

Jake whirled, and shot David. Justin, the physical education teacher, had left the gym when he heard the shot. He tackled Jake, who fell to the floor and dropped the gun. Karen scrambled back to the office, barked at Beatrice to call 911, then announced that the students and teachers were to stay in their classrooms.

David lay on the floor in a pool of blood. While Jake continued to struggle in Justin's grasp, Karen knelt by David.

"You saved my life," she said. "Thank you."

David smiled and slowly closed his eyes. He would never reopen them.

Scripture

John 15:12-17

"This is my commandment, that you love one another as I have loved you. No one has greater love than this, to lay down one's life for one's friends. You are my friends if you do what I command you. I do not call you servants any longer, because the servant does not know what the master is doing; but I have called you friends, because I have made known to you everything that I have heard from my Father. You did not choose me but I chose you. And I appointed you to go and bear fruit, fruit that will last, so that the Father will give you whatever you ask him in my name. I am giving you these commands so that you may love one another."

Sermon

Before he died, Jesus comforted his disciples. He told them he would not leave them orphaned; he would send them the Holy Spirit to advocate for them; he would leave them his peace. He also left them instructions, and some of these were echoes of previous teachings. This passage is a repetition of the Great Commandment, with a new verse: "No one has greater love than this, to lay down one's life for one's friends."

Heroism springs from courage and resourcefulness during a crisis. Whether or not he knew what a risk he was taking, David successfully diverted a bullet intended for his principal, Karen. He received the gunshot himself, and died on the way to the hospital. He saved Karen's life by offering his own.

David had not had an easy life up to this point. His mother had married an alcoholic and was in the process of divorcing him when David entered junior high school. She began to realize that raising her children on her meager wage was more of a burden than she could bear. She lost their house, and for a time, the family had to live in a shelter. Finally, they moved into a low-income housing project. The children were often hungry and were growing out of their clothes.

Karen noticed that David was coming to school in pants that were too short. She collected clothes from neighborhood families and presented them to David's mother. She also connected the family with a food pantry, a financial management class, and Children's Services, which tracked down the estranged father and garnisheed his wages for child support. The family got back on its feet, and David's mother was able to purchase a home.

David revered Karen. He was never embarrassed to wear secondhand clothes. He brought her flowers from his family's garden in the spring and a twelve-pack of pencils at the beginning of the school year. Karen received these gifts graciously.

David responded to Karen's mute call for help just as Karen had perceived his family's need for financial assistance. He risked his life so that danger would be diverted away from his principal. What he didn't know was that this danger would refocus on him and cause his death.

David was as innocent as Jesus Christ as he stood before a crowd that was yelling, "Crucify him!" Christ died for all of humankind, that we might rise to eternal life with him. No greater gift is available to us. No greater love can be experienced.

Prayer

Almighty God,
we are grateful for those
who lay down their lives for their friends.
Especially, we bless you for David,
who bravely defended his principal
and freed his classmates from harm. Amen.

Graveside Prayer

Gracious God,
you give us David's life to cherish.
Help us, as we mourn,
to love one another,
to spend ourselves for one another,
to ward away evil, and to bring about good. Amen.

STUDENT DIES IN HAZING

Context

Sherry always wanted to join a college sorority. Her mom, Elise, had pledged when she was a freshman. When Sherry was a child, Elise would spend hours showing her scrapbooks from college. She loved to retell stories such as how she had met Sherry's father, Dutch, and how his frat brothers had serenaded her when he was ready to give her his pin. Four sorority sisters and Elise's own sister had served as her bridesmaids.

Sherry chose to attend her parents' college. During her freshman year she pledged to her mother's sorority, but she was annoyed at the initiation process. She was told she would have to wear the same outfit, a skirted suit, all week, without washing it or bathing. She would need to carry a sorority sister's books for her and pick up anything she dropped. The sister could call her day or night to demand an errand or service.

Finally, on Friday night, Sherry and the other pledges were led to the basement of one of the fraternity houses. The sister in charge told them they could shower. While they were bathing, some frat brothers entered and confiscated the pledges' clothes. Then the girls learned that another room of the basement had been set up for a sadistic ritual.

Sherry had had enough. She renounced her pledge and attempted to leave the basement wrapped in a towel, but two fraternity brothers prevented her. When she struggled further, a sister said, "Let her go." The brothers refused. They loaded Sherry into the trunk of one of their cars, breaking her collarbone, and sped away.

Moaning in pain, Sherry searched for a trunk release. She didn't find one, but she found a crowbar. She used it to break out one of the taillights. If she could wave to the other drivers, they would know that she was being kidnapped. One of the brothers heard the taillight break and realized that Sherry had damaged his car, so he stopped, flew out of the car, and jerked open the trunk. Sherry, her hands locked around the crowbar, used all of her strength to spring out at him. He seized the crowbar and killed her with a single blow.

The brothers left her on the side of the road. A middle-aged married couple, traveling late that night, found her. Ironically, the woman had been a member of the sorority to which Sherry had pledged. When making a report to the police, she said, "This is truly horrible. We never did this kind of thing."

Scripture

Genesis 37:17b-24

So Joseph went after his brothers, and found them at Dothan. They saw him from a distance, and before he came near to them, they conspired to kill him. They said to one another, "Here comes this dreamer. Come now, let us kill him and throw him into one of the pits; then we shall say that a wild animal has devoured him, and we shall see what will become of his dreams." But when Reuben heard it, he delivered him out of their hands, saying, "Let us not take his life." Reuben said to them, "Shed no blood; throw him into this pit here in the wilderness, but lay no hand on him"—that he might rescue him out of their hand and restore him to his father. So when Joseph came to his brothers, they stripped him of his robe, the long robe with sleeves that he wore; and they took him and threw him into a pit. The pit was empty; there was no water in it.

Sermon

Joseph had a tough life with so many older brothers. Even worse, he was the favorite child of his father Israel, an honor that Joseph's brothers resented. They despised him so much that one day, they plotted to kill him. The only one who disagreed with that plan was Reuben, who insisted instead that they abandon Joseph in a pit. It was from this pit that Joseph was sold into slavery to some Midianites, who took him to Egypt, where he was eventually successful in gaining favor at Pharaoh's court.

The idea behind a process of initiation into a sorority or fraternity is similar to Joseph's life with his brothers. It is a test of fidelity. In Sherry's case, she was a favored child, a legacy, the daughter of a member of the sorority. She would still have to persevere through all of the testing, but her acceptance to the organization was practically automatic.

Sherry's sorority sisters did not make it easy, however. Most of the treatment was standard, but the Friday night ritual was a grim addition to the curriculum. Sherry's response was to leave the scene, and the sister in charge was willing to release her, but two of the brothers would not take no for an answer. Their bravado took them too far, and one lost control. Sherry died from a head injury as she lay by the side of the road.

A pair of Good Samaritans found her, too late to save her. They were so anguished at what happened, they have created a charitable foundation to help families who have lost a loved one to hazing. The foundation will fund advocacy, lobbyists, bereavement services, and education—including self-defense classes for high-school juniors and seniors. With Dutch and Elise's permission this foundation will be named after Sherry.

Sherry sought to join the sorority because she desired relationship. Especially, she wanted to create a network so that she would graduate with both a bachelor's degree and a husband. She had dreams, attainable dreams, just as Joseph had. Like Joseph, her dreams are living on in a different way than she could have predicted. Because of her, campuses will be safer. May we all persevere in helping others realize their dreams, safely.

Prayer

Loving God,
we bless you for Sherry's life,
and for the lives of others
who will be preserved by the Sherry Foundation.
We ask that you might wrap this family
in your powerful arms as they mourn their loss. Amen.

Graveside Prayer

Almighty God,
embolden us to be your people
in relationship with each other,

committed to protecting your children,
resolved in our struggle against violence.
Dismiss us now to serve you in all that we do,
with good will to family and neighbors. Amen.

Student Dies of Untreated Mental Illness

Context

Mike, eighteen, a freshman at a small private college, had trouble adjusting to his new life. He had come to school as a meek young man, hoping to quietly study for a bachelor's degree. Instead, he'd transformed into a party animal, drinking until late at night and skipping class the next morning. When it came time to study for midterm exams, he stayed up all night reading the texts that he'd neglected. His written work made no sense, however, and he failed two of his five classes.

Mike's academic advisor asked him to stop by his office. When the advisor asked him what had happened, Mike couldn't speak a straight sentence. Knowing that something must be wrong, the advisor asked Mike to go see his general practitioner. Mike said he would, but instead he drove to the nearest large city for an afternoon drink. On his way back to his dormitory, he called his father on his cellular phone to let him know he was quitting school. In the midst of this conversation, Mike veered off the road, crashed through a guardrail and plummeted into the river below. A passing motorist witnessed the accident and called the local police. The police called an ambulance, which sped Mike to a nearby hospital. He was pronounced dead on arrival.

An autopsy confirmed not only a high level of intoxication, but also a chemical imbalance. Mike had been experiencing a series of manic-depressive episodes, which he had self-treated with alcohol. Crestfallen, Mike's father called you with the news. He asked you to officiate at the funeral.

Scripture

Matthew 13:24-30

He put before them another parable: "The kingdom of heaven may be compared to someone who sowed good seed in his field; but while everybody was asleep, an enemy came and sowed weeds among the wheat, and then went away. So when the plants came up and bore grain, then the weeds appeared as well. And the slaves of the householder came and said to him, 'Master, did you not sow good seed in your field? Where, then did these weeds come from?' He answered, 'An enemy has done this.' The slaves said to him, 'Then do you want us to go and gather them?' But he replied, 'No; for in gathering the weeds you would uproot the wheat along with them. Let both of them grow together until the harvest; and at harvest time I will tell the reapers, Collect the weeds first and bind them in bundles to be burned, but gather the wheat into my barn.'"

Sermon

In God's economy, nothing is wasted. The weeds grow up among the wheat and then are sorted out at harvest. They are bundled to be burned, and then the wheat is gathered to be ground into flour and made into bread.

All of us have weeds in our character. We may not be conscious of all of them. Some weeds are illnesses; some are sin; some are longings for things we may never have. These weeds grow up with the better part of our character, the wheat. Ordinarily, we make good decisions despite the weeds, and the wheat in us matures to full fruition. It is used to feed ourselves, our families, and others. In certain individuals, at times, the weeds take over and cause poor judgment. The poor judgment can lead to accidents, even death. This is what happened to Mike.

Mike was the quiet boy in Sunday school class. He exhibited all of the fruits of the Holy Spirit—love, joy, peace, patience, generosity, kindness, and self-control. He honored his mother and father. His teenage years brought discernment in his loyalty to friends so that his parents never had trouble with his associations. He was a good boy and promised to be a fine young man.

But during his later years of schooling, some weeds were growing in his mind. Their effects weren't immediately obvious. A chemical imbalance was developing in Mike's brain. By the time he arrived at college, the conditions were already ripe for an episode. His new situation was sufficiently upsetting as to set off a radical change of behavior. The weeds grew quickly and took over, causing poor judgment and an accident that led to Mike's death.

Now we are mourning the loss of an otherwise healthy young man, who died of a treatable disease. We are shocked and angry. We are bewildered. As Mike's father has said, "I expected Mike to bury me. Now I'm burying him." Mike's family is grieving, and life will never be the same.

So where is God's justice? We have learned a bitter lesson about loving one another. We now know to watch each other, especially our young men and women, for uncharacteristic behaviors. We now know that the weeds of our character can take over when we find ourselves overcome by the stress of change. This lesson will not be wasted on us.

This might satisfy our minds, but what about our hearts? The God of Abraham, Isaac, and Jacob is still on the throne. God cannot be moved. The Word of the Lord is true and God's commandments are firm. God is weeping with us now, as he holds out his arms in compassion to Mike, who has entered the heavenly throne room. May God grant us such a vision of resurrection.

Prayer

Almighty God,
we are grateful for Mike's life,
both the weeds and the wheat.
Bless him with peace.
Grant him your mercy.
Accept him into your arms. Amen.

Graveside Prayer

Gracious God,
let us live our lives boldly,
praising your name in your sanctuary

and loving one another with compassion.
Give us energy and strength
to help one another through difficulties,
especially Mike's family in their grief. Amen.

STUDENT DIES OF ACCIDENTAL OVERDOSE

Context

Roderick, a college freshman from a township in rural Ohio, left home early in September, his car loaded with clothes and electronics. He was free at last. He would no longer have an enforced bedtime. He would not have to do early morning chores. He could enjoy the company of his friends all weekend. He could attend classes or not.

Orientation at State University was pizza, wings, games, and hilarity. After hours, there was more beer than at Oktoberfest. Rod soon acquainted himself with the charms of chemical detachment. He also got to know some congenial young women.

Finally the amusements had to stop and the studying had to start, but Rod was lost in his engineering classes. None of his high school coursework had prepared him for the mysteries of process synthesis. After midterm exams, he and his roommate Ben sought chemical comfort.

Since they didn't know where to buy illegal drugs and couldn't afford them, they visited the corner drug store and purchased some cough syrup with dextromethorphan bromide. They sat in their dorm room, each with a bottle, and chugged. Then they each sipped another bottle. By midnight, they had slipped into permanent sleep.

Rod's family found them the next day when they came to visit. In cold shock, Rod's father called you to ask you to do a funeral for what appeared to be his son's suicide. The deaths were later ruled accidental by the county coroner.

Scripture

Luke 15:11-24

Then Jesus said, "There was a man who had two sons. The younger of them said to his father, 'Father, give me the share of the property that will belong to me.' So he divided his property between them. A few days later the younger son gathered all he had and traveled to a distant country, and there he squandered his property in dissolute living. When he had spent everything, a severe famine took place throughout that country, and he began to be in need. So he went and hired himself out to one of the citizens of that country, who sent him to his fields to feed the pigs. He would gladly have filled himself with the pods that the pigs were eating; and no one gave him anything. But when he came to himself, he said, 'How many of my father's hired hands have bread enough and to spare, but here I am dying of hunger! I will get up and go to my father, and I will say to him, "Father, I have sinned against heaven and before you; I am no longer worthy to be called your son; treat me like one of your hired hands."' So he set off and went to his father. But while he was still far off, his father saw him and was filled with compassion; he ran and put his arms around him and kissed him. Then the son said to him, 'Father, I have sinned against heaven and before you. I am no longer worthy to be called your son.' But the father said to his slaves, 'Quickly, bring out a robe—the best one—and put it on him; put a ring on his finger and sandals on his feet. And get the fatted calf and kill it, and let us eat and celebrate; for this son of mine was dead and is alive again; he was lost and is found!' And they began to celebrate."

Sermon

The parable of the Prodigal Son is a story about the unconditional love of a father for his wayward son, even after his son does the unforgivable. The parable includes the story of a jealous brother who cannot understand why his father would celebrate the return of this son who had squandered his fortune. The first part of the story, however, most closely resembles the preceding two stories in this chapter—the parable of the Lost Sheep and the parable of the Lost Coin. In each, that which was lost was found again, to the great joy of everyone concerned.

Roderick, like most children, had had his share of getting lost. At the state fair one year, he wandered off to try an amusement park ride. The rest of his family was headed toward the grandstand. When they discovered that he was gone, they retraced their steps, calling his name. Finally, they had him paged over the public address system. Reunited, they celebrated with hugs and Belgian waffles before attending the tractor pull.

The family has been close. They enjoy an excellent reputation in this rural community. They prize their seventy head of dairy cattle, and are all hard workers. Until he left to go to State University, Rod helped milk the herd, fix the equipment, harvest the grain crops, and supervise the younger boys.

He was a good student. He got As and Bs, with an occasional C in the more arcane subjects, such as French and Latin. He had mastered American English, and that was enough for him.

Rod was proud to be the first person in his family to attend college. He chose engineering as a major because he liked the sound of it. He knew it involved science and math. He was good at those subjects.

When he arrived at his first class, however, the professor seemed to speak a different language. At State University, freshmen are exposed to the most difficult courses first. If they pass muster, they can try the rest.

Rod was as lost as he was at the State Fair. Both he and his roommate Ben were experiencing the horror of flunking a class in their freshman year. They tried to make it look like they knew what they were doing. Their phone conversations with their families were positive, even buoyant. But when the midterm scores came back, both of them knew they were failing. Their hopes were scattered.

To ease the pain, they turned to chemical experimentation. They both knew the properties of dextromethorphan bromide, an ingredient in cough syrup. They *didn't* know their limits. Further and further into their experiment, their judgment became impaired. They died in their dormitory at State University, both lost in the search for freedom from pain.

The parable of the Prodigal Son ends happily. The lost son reunites with his father the king, and even though his older brother isn't happy about it, everyone else celebrates. If we think of God as the king, and Rod and Ben as sons, we can imagine how they entered heaven. There was a joyous celebration. Even though these two young men are lost to us, they are found in heaven, and all who have gone before them are more than happy to receive them. God has put rings on their fingers and robes on their backs. God has killed the fatted calf, and the celebration has begun. They are home in the heavens, free of the pain that defeated them.

Now we feel pain, a longing for Rod and Ben, an aching for relief from this sorrow. For those of us who were close to them, we may feel lost for quite a while. We might shake our heads in disbelief, sob as though we'll never stop, or become so depressed we don't want to eat. But God our King is always willing to receive us when we come back from our wanderings. God is always ready to hear our prayers. God spreads his arms, shouts a welcome, and takes us back, no matter how far we have strayed.

Prayer

O God our King,
you care deeply for us.
You lead us through pitched battles.
You shout encouragement.
You send people to tend our wounds.
Bless us with your mercy, we pray,
for we are lost without your leadership.
Amen.

Graveside Prayer

Everlasting God,
you have created us to be strong.
You have given us purpose and drive.

But sometimes, we need to stop
to reflect on your goodness,
to partake of your unconditional love.
Be a real presence for us in the coming days.
May we find you in one another's embrace.
Amen.

CHAPTER FOUR

ADULTS

ADULT DIES OF SERIOUS ILLNESS

Context

Leilani, thirty-eight, restaurant and bar owner, had constant migraines for several weeks. She tried analgesics, relaxation massage, cold compresses, and warm baths. Nothing worked. Her daughter Lila insisted that she go to their internist.

The doctor did a thorough examination, arranged for some tests, and asked Leilani to come back in one week. When the test results returned, they showed a metastasis of brain cancer.

Surgery revealed the extent of the metastasis. Leilani bravely withstood the treatment prescribed, which included daily radiation treatments for four weeks and four months of chemotherapy. Each treatment made her a bit weaker. She knew her family was having difficulty caring for her. She consented to home health care and hospice. Her husband Mark sold the restaurant to a family friend, who kept the name, Leilani's Grass Skirt Grille.

Scripture

Luke 24:50-53

Then he led them out as far as Bethany, and, lifting up his hands, he blessed them. While he was blessing them, he withdrew from them and was carried up into heaven. And they worshiped him, and returned to Jerusalem with great joy; and they were continually in the temple blessing God.

Sermon

Our Lord Jesus Christ did tremendous service for the people around him and for the public at large. He taught, preached, healed people, and ate with sinners and tax collectors. He did the unanticipated. Jesus sat and spoke with a woman at a well, in a land where most Jews would not even consider stopping to refresh themselves.

When Jesus died, despite his teaching about his resurrection, his disciples thought all was lost. They were so despondent that Jesus returned to see them again, to offer one more teaching on his resurrection, according to the scriptures. Then he rose to leave, lifting his hands, and began his ascension to heaven while he was still blessing them.

Leilani died while she was still blessing her family, her friends, and the customers of her restaurant, Leilani's Grass Skirt Grille. Up until a year ago, she was the vibrant loving woman we had all come to know. As her health declined, she was still vocal in her love for all who came to visit her and all who cared for her. With Lila's help, she sent out one hundred fifty Christmas cards with hula girls on the front.

Leilani was a rare person. She radiated sunshine, and she loved to give joy to others. When she set up a Hawaiian-themed restaurant in Minnesota, no one wondered why. People flocked to partake of the foods and beverages of an exotic land. Leilani decorated her restaurant authentically, from the torch lamps outside to the little umbrellas in the drinks. She would wait table, tend bar, and engage in banter with the customers, always wearing her traditional grass skirt.

Leilani paid special attention to those who came to her restaurant alone. She'd see them at the bar or the lunch counter. She would fill their order personally, giving them all of the attention due to an honored guest. If anyone left her a huge tip, she would share it with the staff. In the same way, if the restaurant made an exceptional profit, she would split it among those who worked with her. She closed the restaurant down twice per year to throw parties for the staff.

She was generous to the last. Even when she was leaving this earth, she wanted her daughter Lila to know how much their relationship had meant to her, so she mustered her strength and tried to speak the words Lila had so often heard from her. When she could no longer speak them, Lila finished her sentence for her. "I know, Mom. I love you too." Then Leilani breathed her last.

Leilani died young, leaving a family, a swirl of friends, and an avid clientele. Like Jesus, she left us while she was still blessing us, still giving much of herself, still radiating sunshine. And like Jesus, she has a group of followers who will maintain her tradition, that all may bask in the warmth of Hawaii in the frigid plains of Minnesota.

Prayer

Gracious God,
we are grateful for the love and joy
that you brought to us through Leilani.
We ask that you will keep us close to each other,
that our mutual memories may continue to
enhance our lives.
May we encourage each other. Amen.

Graveside Prayer

Loving God,
you give us wonderful people to cherish.
Let Leilani's memory radiate for us like the sun,

and may her example inspire us all
to give joy to people we know, and people we don't
know. Amen.

Adult Dies in Prison

Context

Donna had spent more than half of her forty-six years in prison. She killed her husband when she was twenty-two years old, three years after they married. At the time, she had thought she was acting in self-defense, but her husband's family had hired two of the state's best attorneys. The judge sentenced her to twenty-five years in prison.

Imprisonment was difficult for Donna, not only because her children were distant but also because the prison was a hotbed of disease. Prone to sinus infections and bronchitis, Donna's suffering began immediately. Recently, a bout with pneumonia had landed her in the infirmary. The head nurse called you to let you know that Donna might not have much longer to live. You responded by registering yourself as her clergy of record and going to visit her at the next scheduled visiting hour.

Donna was resting when you entered her room. A tube had been inserted in her nose to drain fluid, but she was still able to converse. Donna had received much help from the prison chaplain and a visiting psychologist. Her children had kept up a steady, encouraging correspondence.

After twenty minutes with her, she had told you her history; and during the rest of the hour, she spoke her confession. At the end of the visiting period, you affirmed her and said a prayer with her. She died peacefully that night. Her family asked you to officiate at her funeral.

Scripture

Luke 19:1-10

[Jesus] entered Jericho and was passing through it. A man was there named Zacchaeus; he was a chief tax collector and was rich. He was trying to see who Jesus was, but on account of the crowd he could not, because he was short in stature. So he ran ahead and climbed a sycamore tree to see him, because he was going to pass that way. When Jesus came to the place, he looked up and said to him, "Zacchaeus, hurry and come down; for I must stay at your house today." So he hurried down and was happy to welcome him. All who saw it began to grumble and said, "He has gone to be the guest of one who is a sinner." Zacchaeus stood there and said to the Lord, "Look, half of my possessions, Lord, I will give to the poor; and if I have defrauded anyone of anything, I will pay back four times as much." Then Jesus said to him, "Today salvation has come to this house, because he too is a son of Abraham. For the Son of Man came to seek out and to save the lost."

Sermon

Jesus came to seek out sinners, to eat with tax collectors, and to reunite the people of Israel. As he began to encounter people in need, his mission grew to include teaching and healing. His ministry to the sick, the lonely, and the evildoer made him unpopular among certain onlookers. They criticized his ministry and alerted the authorities. Toward the end of his life, he was not only prevented from doing good works but also treated as a criminal himself.

When Jesus encountered Zacchaeus, he was in Jericho, on his way to his final destination, Jerusalem. By the time this man hailed him from a tree, Jesus had already healed lepers, preached to multitudes, and prepared his disciples for his death. It was typical of Jesus to eat with sinners. What was unusual was the immediate and spontaneous repentance and restitution offered by Zacchaeus for his sin. Jesus accepted him as a child of Abraham, and proclaimed his mission to the lost.

Donna lay sick in prison with pneumonia. She had long ago repented of the sin for which she was serving hard time. She had long ago accepted the Lord. But she needed some help facing her death. Although the prison chaplain had been helpful in the past, Donna asked me, a member of her home community, to listen to her story.

This woman spent the best years of her life in prison. She had led a good life among the other prisoners. She had prayed her best prayers, for herself and for others. She had led a Bible study. She was able to do all things through Christ who strengthened her. Last Christmas, the chaplain asked her to light the Christ candle.

Like Zacchaeus, Donna's conversion was complete. When she entered the prison, she had been among the lost, an onlooker to Christianity. By the time she spoke her truth to me, she had been found. She had even been seeking out the lost herself, praying for them and bringing them to the Lord. And the Lord accepted her as a daughter of God, one who had made the best of a bad situation.

It is never too late in our lives to turn to the Lord and forsake sin. No sin is too terrible to confess to the Lord, for God is good, and his steadfast love endures forever. Donna could have lived a life of desperation, but she chose the way, the truth, and the life. Wherever we need to make restitution, wherever we need to seek the lost—even in a tree, wherever we need to listen to a voice in need, let us do good and avoid evil.

Prayer

Loving God,
we are grateful for all of Donna's good works,
and for the high esteem in which she was held.
We bless you for all those who seek the lost
in forbidding places.
We ask you to empower us to do likewise. Amen.

Graveside Prayer

Gracious God,
help us all our lives through
to seek the lost, and bring them to you.
Look kindly on our efforts,

in the name of the one
who ate with tax collectors and sinners. Amen.

Adult Completes Suicide

Context

Tad, thirty-six, was the loving father of three boys. He coached their Little League team. He took them to and from soccer practice. He cooked their meals and picked them up from school. His wife Catherine, thirty-two, was an accountant and a paralegal. She was the main breadwinner of the family.

Tad helped out with snow removal and home repairs for the elderly in the neighborhood, but he had been unable to hold down a steady job since his own father died seven years before. Since that time, he had been clinically depressed. Despite Catherine's insistence that he seek help, Tad had remained untreated.

Catherine came home one night to announce that she'd found a position as managing principal accountant in a firm more than five hundred miles away. She had been conducting a national job search, unbeknownst to Tad. She would assume her duties a week from the following Monday.

"What about the boys?" asked Tad.

"The moving truck is coming 8:00 a.m. Monday. The packers will arrive this Saturday. The boys are going with me."

"Then, what about me?"

"You're not going, Tad. Here." Catherine served him with divorce papers and whisked out of the house to go to her second job.

That evening, it was all Tad could do not to let on to the boys what was happening. With relief, he tucked them in bed. Alone, with hands shaking, he read the papers. It was all there, legal and succinct. As Tad came to a full realization of the situation, his hope vanished.

Late that night, Catherine arrived in her darkened home. One stream of light shone from the bathroom lighting fixture. Tad lay in the bathtub, his jugular and carotid arteries severed by a straight razor which dangled from his right hand. A suicide note read, "The pain was too great. I decided to have it all at once. O God, I'm sorry."

Catherine called you and the funeral director within a minute and a half. Then she collapsed on the living room sofa, sobbing.

Scripture

Luke 15:3-7

So he told them this parable: "Which one of you, having a hundred sheep and losing one of them, does not leave the ninety-nine in the wilderness and go after the one that is lost until he finds it? When he has found it, he lays it on his shoulders and rejoices. And when he comes home, he calls together his friends and neighbors, saying to them, 'Rejoice with me, for I have found my sheep that was lost.' Just so, I tell you, there will be more joy in heaven over one sinner who repents than over ninety-nine righteous persons who need no repentance."

Sermon

Jesus looked out for the lost. He had a heart for the despised, the sinners, and the tax collectors. He told people that he came for the sick among us, for the healthy have no need of a doctor.

Jesus loves Tad. For him, Tad was like a sheep that had lost its way. Through Catherine, he tried to bring Tad to the light. Catherine encouraged him to find help through mental health resources. She had even given him phone numbers of those persons whom others had recommended. But Tad was too lost to listen to reason. He needed the Lord himself.

On the night that Tad completed suicide, Jesus left the ninety-nine righteous ones and went to seek the lost. He waded through the swamps of Tad's despair and called to him. Had someone been at Tad's side to speak Jesus' words, he may have heard the voice of a friend. But he had asked no one for support. He tucked his boys into bed, and then he was alone with his pain. He hurt so deeply that he felt he had to harm himself to be free. Catherine's husband, the father of Adam, Michael, and Thomas, died at his own hand.

Unwilling to leave a sheep lost, Jesus still sought him. He knelt at Tad's side, trying to help. Tad was in Gethsemane, and Jesus was with him. But Tad couldn't see him. He couldn't see anything. He could feel only the pain of loss. He wrote his note and took his own life, leaving Jesus anguished but still fully committed to Tad.

Jesus picked up his sheep and carried him to God. He laid him at God's feet, and they both wept. At length, God said, "Prepare him a room." Then Tad rose, in his right mind, with a new body, and worshiped God. The heavenly host surrounded him, singing spiritual songs. Among those rejoicing was Tad's father, Tom.

For Catherine, Adam, Michael, and Thomas, a new day has dawned. It is a day of numbness that may turn into bitterness, and may give way to anger, and finally, acceptance. Wherever they travel, this family will need the support of a church. May they find all they need where they're going. They will certainly have our prayerful support.

Prayer

Eternal Father,
we are grateful for the persistence of Jesus,
who taught us to leave the ninety-nine
to seek the lost.
For Tad, grant everlasting peace.
For his family, grant strong faith. Amen.

Graveside Prayer

Gracious God,
help us to live our lives in search of the lost.
Let us be like your son, the good shepherd,
vigilant and persistent

in the care of your flock.
May we live as your people
die in your service, and rise in your presence, rejoicing.
Amen.

Adult Dies in Random Act of Violence

Context

Twenty-nine-year-old Kaylee had finally met the man she wanted to marry. Ray was rich, handsome, and strong, and he had a penchant for traveling. He loved to hop on a plane to go to lunch in a major city and then come back in time for an evening round of golf. Kaylee and Ray met when she was serving cocktails to the first-class passengers, and they had struck up a conversation. It was her night off, so they had dinner. They continued to date for a year, and then Ray proposed marriage.

Their wedding day came, and Kaylee was bedecked in satin and pearls. The ceremony went perfectly, and they were off to their reception, which was held at a redecorated airplane hangar. The flight strip was still available for takeoffs, so Ray arranged for a plane to pick them up and fly them to a small island known for its honeymoon retreats.

As they arrived at the island the next day, the couple didn't notice from the air that the inhabitants were experiencing some unrest. The plane landed, and Ray and Kaylee were expecting to deplane, but there was no landing crew to wheel the stairs to the aircraft. "You'll have to get off," said the pilot. "I'm picking up another couple in a half-hour."

Ray and Kaylee rose to comply, but at that moment, a shot rang out. They all hit the floor, but Kaylee was already bleeding from her temple. She was mortally wounded. Ray insisted that the pilot fly her to the next island for medical treatment, but by the time they arrived, it was too late.

Ray called you, since you had performed their wedding, and you were the only preacher he knew. He asked you to officiate at Kaylee's memorial service.

Scripture

John 10:11-18

"I am the good shepherd. The good shepherd lays down his life for the sheep. The hired hand, who is not the shepherd and does not own the sheep, sees the wolf coming and leaves the sheep and runs away—and the wolf snatches them and scatters them. The hired hand runs away because a hired hand does not care for the sheep. I am the good shepherd. I know my own and my own know me, just as the Father knows me and I know the Father. And I lay down my life for the sheep. I have other sheep that do not belong to this fold. I must bring them also, and they will listen to my voice. So there will be one flock, one shepherd. For this reason the Father loves me, because I lay down my life in order to take it up again. No one takes it from me, but I lay it down of my own accord. I have power to lay it down, and I have power to take it up again. I have received this command from my Father."

Sermon

Jesus has often been compared with the good shepherd, the one who would lay down his life for his sheep. We hear the same description of Jesus in the verse, "No one has greater love than this, to lay down one's life for one's friends" (John 15:13). Jesus died on the cross for our salvation and rose to heaven to show us the way into God's heart.

Kaylee unwittingly took a bullet to save Ray and the pilot of the aircraft that flew them to their honeymoon. In a sense, she put herself in harm's way and saved both men from certain death. She was a victim of a random act of violence, sprung from a wave of political unrest no one involved could have foreseen.

What Ray may not have known about Kaylee before she married him was that she was a Christian. She had grown up at our church. She had attended Sunday school from an early age. She was the secretary's assistant for many years, and she substituted for the secretary when she was on vacation. When she came of age, she fulfilled a lifetime ambition to go to school and become a flight attendant on an international airline. In that way she was able to see the world and give people comfort as they traveled.

When she came to see me after she met Ray, I knew something special had happened even before she began to tell the story. Her face radiated joy. Her usual neat and organized look became a little more casual. When she and Ray attended church one Sunday and he stood up with her to make an announcement, it was no surprise to me. I was honored to officiate at their wedding.

I knew that Kaylee would take her wedding vows seriously, but I'm sure no one at her wedding could have foreseen this immediate and tragic outcome. Having known Jesus Christ, she followed in his footsteps, right to the last. We honor her today, as we honored both her and Ray only a few days ago. May all of us take our commitments as seriously.

Prayer

Almighty God,
we are grateful for Kaylee and her commitment to Ray.
Bless us all as we mourn our loss,
and help us to take up our role
as shepherds of one another. Amen.

Graveside Prayer

Gracious God,
you give us wonderful people to love.
We praise you for Kaylee,
your servant and our joy.
Guard our hearts as we learn to live courageously, as she did.
Amen.

Adult Dies in Work Accident

Context

Joe, forty-five, loved his work. He was an architect who had designed several of the buildings in one of the larger cities in his state. He drafted each of his projects meticulously, presented his plans, and then made a final blueprint for the builders. He wasn't satisfied, however, until he had witnessed the pouring of the foundation. He would visit again as the building took form. He visited, not as a petulant artist, but as one in awe of the whole process of creation.

On one of these visits, Joe watched a crew building a community recreation and fitness complex. He received a call on his cell phone from a worker who asked him to look at a development on the other side of the building. Joe jumped into a four-wheeler and sped away. As he was rounding a corner, he encountered a dump truck. Swerving to miss it, he upended the four-wheeler. It landed on top of him, and he was crushed by its weight. Even though an ambulance came within minutes, Joe died on the worksite.

Joe's wife Charlotte called you as a neighbor drove her to the site. She requested pastoral care and your leadership of a memorial service for Joe.

Scripture

Ecclesiastes 3:9-15

What gain have the workers from their toil? I have seen the business that God has given to everyone to be busy with. He has made everything suitable for its time; moreover he has put a sense of past and future into their minds, yet they cannot find out what God has done from the beginning to the end. I know that there is nothing better for them than to be happy and enjoy themselves as long as they live; moreover, it is God's gift that all should eat and drink and take pleasure in all their toil. I know that whatever God does endures forever; nothing can be added to it, nor anything taken from it; God has done this, so that all should stand in awe before him. That which is, already has been; that which is to be, already is; and God seeks out what has gone by.

Sermon

The writer of Ecclesiastes was a sophisticated, wise person, one who had lived through much, one who had come to learn many things by experience and by listening to others. This writer had an appreciation of the divine view of human happiness. Eating, drinking, and working are some of the most satisfying ways we pursue happiness.

This writer must have had a friend like Joe. Seldom have I encountered someone who loved to work more than Joe. He landed several city government contracts due to his fine attitude and excellent workmanship in designing buildings. He even tried his hand at planning a topiary park for the city, a design that earned him the prestigious National Design Award.

Our city is known for its architecture, and Joe did a fine job matching the lines and structure of the new buildings he designed with the original courthouse, post office, and county seat building. We can only imagine how happy the founders were to witness the continuation of their proud tradition.

Joe's spirit flew up to heaven when he tried to avoid a collision and his four-wheeler spun out of control. For a brief moment, he was in pain; then he entered eternal peace and luxury. We can only imagine how happy were the founders, and Jesus himself, to greet Joe in God's huge mansion beyond the clouds. They may already have him designing a new building for other new arrivals in heaven.

For Charlotte and her children, we offer our deepest sympathy. We know that when such a dynamic man dies, he leaves a cavern of loneliness. None of us can fill the void left by the loss of a loving father. We can help the family adjust to what is, for now. Joe's friends in the city government have already offered legal advocacy and financial help. The church stands ready with love and support.

Joe was a man of faith, and had a good knowledge of the scriptures. I was with him at a worksite one day, and I saw his face crinkle into a smile as some workers poured the foundation for a new building. The mixer backed up to the building site, and the concrete poured out like molten lava. He said, "See that? Now, when that dries, that will be like the house built on a rock."

"A firm foundation?" I asked.

"The *best*!" he enthused, grinning at me broadly. Just before we pulled away from the site, he wrote a few notes on his clipboard. Then he grabbed his cell phone from his belt and called the driver of the concrete truck to say, "Good job! Thank you!"

May God bless us all as we live the scriptures, as Joe did, and as we encourage each other through this heartbreaking loss.

Prayer

Loving God,
how firm is our foundation
when we trust in you.
We bless you for Joe's life,
especially his enthusiasm for work.
We ask your care for his family,
and your protection for all of those assembled
here. Amen.

Graveside Prayer

Gracious God,
you give us your love all day long.
You seem especially close to us
as we mourn here today.
Grant us wisdom and energy
as we find every reason to care for each other.
Amen.

Chapter Five

Older Adults

Older Adult Dies in Nursing Home

Context

Abigail sits in her wheelchair, her hand supporting her head. Seventy-seven years old, she is suffering from end-stage dementia. Occasionally, her elbow slips from the armrest, and she awakens, frightened. If one of the nurse's aides notices, she comes to console her a moment, then leaves abruptly to care for another patient.

When she was thirty years younger, Abigail became a state legislator. She held several political offices while maintaining a legal practice. She was the sole support of her only child, Heather, while Heather was growing up. Her husband, a police officer, had been shot and killed while on duty in their midsize town.

Heather profited from her mother's industry, but she resented her political career. She felt as if she lived in a fishbowl. She was never so happy as the day she moved away to attend college. After graduation, she severed ties. She did not invite her mother to her wedding. She did not attend her mother's inauguration to state office.

Heather had started to attend your church when her mother's health was failing. You encouraged her to visit her mother and offered to accompany her. When Abigail died six months later, Heather asked you to officiate at her funeral.

Scripture

Luke 18:1-8

Then Jesus told them a parable about their need to pray always and not to lose heart. He said, "In a certain city there was a judge who neither feared God nor had respect for people. In that city there was a widow who kept coming to him and saying, 'Grant me justice against my opponent.' For a while he refused; but later he said to himself, 'Though I have no fear of God and no respect for anyone, yet because this widow keeps bothering me, I will grant her justice, so that she may not wear me out by continually coming.'" And the Lord said, "Listen to what the unjust judge says. And will not God grant justice to his chosen ones who cry to him day and night? Will he delay long in helping them? I tell you, he will quickly grant justice to them. And yet, when the Son of Man comes, will he find faith on earth?"

Sermon

God answers prayer, sometimes sooner, sometimes later—always in God's own time. The persistent widow was one who darkened the door of the unjust judge many a time before he granted her justice. How much easier it is for us to pray to God for the fulfillment of our needs. God always listens to us with great compassion.

As the widow persisted, so did Abigail. Her prayers availed much. Widowed at age thirty-six, she strove to support her daughter Heather through the rest of high school and college. She found a unique way to do that. She ran for public office.

Abigail started on the city council, and then advanced to chancellor. She was interim mayor after Harold Roberts stepped down midterm. In the last months of her interim term, she ran as the incumbent, and she won. To complete her career, she spent seventeen years in the state legislature.

But something was missing for Abigail during those years. When Heather left for college out of state, she was no longer in her mother's jurisdiction. Although Abigail tried to contact her daughter, her efforts failed. She even hired a private investigator at one point, to no avail.

Then she tried prayer. She filled a notebook with written prayers for her daughter's health and prosperity. She asked God to bring the two of them back together. She imagined their reunion in her mind before rising every morning. They hadn't spoken to each other until recently, when Heather began visiting Abigail at her nursing facility.

The renewal of their relationship was the answer to Abigail's prayers. By the look on Abigail's face, Heather perceived that all of Abigail's years had been erased, and a new day had begun. Although she couldn't speak, Abigail was able to express her joy at the return of her daughter. Heather returned to visit every week for six months. She engaged a hospice nurse to ensure that her mother was well cared for in her last days.

Abigail was persistent in her prayer. When her husband died, her hope was to raise her daughter. After Heather left home, Abigail's fondest wish was to be reunited with her. She was not deterred by the unread, returned letters; unanswered phone calls; or e-mail that hung in cyberspace.

When we persist in petitioning God, God will answer, sometimes by granting our desires, other times by changing our hearts. Heather, knowingly or not, answered God's call to visit her mother. And that gave both of them much joy.

As we celebrate Abigail's life, we not only admire her political career but we also rejoice that she never lost heart in prayer. May we go and do likewise.

Prayer

Almighty God,
we are grateful for Abigail,
especially, for her persistence in prayer.

We rejoice in her reunion with her daughter.
We praise you for all of her help
to the people of this state.
We ask your blessing on us as we mourn our loss,
and rejoice in her entry into life everlasting. Amen.

Graveside Prayer

Gracious God,
you summon us to love one another.
You give us the attentiveness to hear
the calling of each other's hearts.
You help us to know the height and depth of love
by calling us into your heart.
May we grow well and do right in your name. Amen.

Older Adult Dies of Serious Illness

Context

Hazel, eighty-seven, sat alone in the common area of her nursing facility, listing over the side of her wheelchair. Her feet, clad in slipper socks, dangled toward the floor. She was nonverbal and noncommunicative, except for an occasional expletive. She was combative. The staff at the facility had difficulty bathing and changing her.

Hazel had been suffering from end-stage dementia for two years when you met her family. You offered to accompany Hal, one of her sons, on a visit, but he resisted. "I can only go every so often," he said. Seeing his mother in this condition upset him too much. His mother's hospice chaplain visited her regularly. He offered to involve you in Hazel's care.

Her son told you that his mother had led an impulsive life. She had quit high school in her last year to elope with John, two years her senior. She had moved with him to the East Coast, where they worked for one of his friends at a tavern. After two months Hazel quit, saying the work was too hard. She became pregnant with the first of five children. She began buying enough nursery furnishings and maternity clothes for every young mother on their block. Creditors began to call, demanding payment. John took a second job. He instructed Hazel to pay only cash.

A postpartum depression landed Hazel in a mental institution. She would live in and out of such facilities for the rest of her life, despite the joy she experienced in motherhood. When she was well, Hazel loved to participate in her children's school activities as room mother or chaperone. She enjoyed baking, particularly at Christmastime, when she would engage her children in decorating sugar cookies.

Hazel died at 2:00 a.m. Christmas morning. The hospice chaplain attended her death. He had called her sons and daughters on Christmas Eve; all but Hal were either unable or unwilling to come. At the moment of her death, Hazel sat up in bed and opened her eyes and raised her arms, as if to welcome someone. Then she lay down again and breathed her last.

Scripture

Deuteronomy 34:1-5

Then Moses went up from the plains of Moab to Mount Nebo, to the top of Pisgah, which is opposite Jericho, and the LORD showed him the whole land: Gilead as far as Dan, all Naphtali, the land of Ephraim and Manasseh, all the land of Judah as far as the Western Sea, the Negeb, and the Plain—that is, the valley of Jericho, the city of palm trees—as far as Zoar. The LORD said to him, "This is the land of which I swore to Abraham, to Isaac, and to Jacob, saying, 'I will give it to your descendants'; I have let you see it with your eyes, but you shall not cross over there." Then Moses, the servant of the LORD, died there in the land of Moab, at the LORD's command.

Sermon

Moses died a beautiful death. The Lord showed him the vision of all that his people would inherit because of him. He received a brief glimpse of all he had worked so hard to gain for God's people. He was filled with glory, awe-stricken, and humbled. After that one brilliant moment, he died at the Lord's command.

Among the Jewish leaders, none had as hard a life as Moses. Ordered by God—against his will—to lead his people out of slavery from Egypt, criticized bitterly by his followers, and pursued by Pharaoh's army, Moses surmounted many obstacles. Even so, his people scorned him as often as they revered him.

Hazel followed in Moses's example. She died a beautiful death, holding out her arms to receive the Lord even when she was far too weak to do so. Her son Hal and her hospice chaplain were there at her side, incredulous. Hazel had endured tremendous adversity in her life. During some years, she had experienced more illness than wellness. Despite all of her disease and heartache, she was still able to raise five children.

In the moment before her life ended, God showed her the promised land. We can imagine that it was a heaven full of luxury and comfort—a banquet table laden with food, pearly gates and golden streets, and loving family members who had gone before her—everything she had dreamed. She wanted to go just as Moses wanted to go, obedient to the Lord's command. She welcomed the Lord into her arms and spirited away with him.

Hazel left five children behind, who now must deal with her loss. When Moses left the Israelites, they wept for thirty days. Hazel's children are likely to weep for months but their weeping will be interspersed with remembrance. Gradually, each of them will return to work and start enjoying the same pastimes in which they had formerly been involved. They will be the persons they always have been, but perhaps with a little more wisdom and a bit more compassion.

It is difficult to grow up with a mother who struggles with illness. Sometimes Hazel's children did not know what to expect from one day to the next. They knew their mother well enough, however, to understand that she loved them, even though at times she lost her ability to express her love.

May we go from here in appreciation of a woman who gave all she had to give, in all the ways she could give. May we go and do the same.

Prayer

Gracious God,
you have given us a wonderful woman to love.
You have matured us by our relationship with her.
You have given us wisdom and compassion.
Bless us in our grief,
and draw us closer to you. Amen.

Graveside Prayer

Everlasting God,
help us through these days to come
to be your people,
strong in our faith,
bold to speak your Word,
true to your command
to love one another. Amen.

Older Adult Dies Alone

Context

Georgia, sixty-six, had lived alone since her husband's death three years before. The couple had anticipated a retirement of travel, volunteerism, and entertaining grandchildren when he died of a massive heart attack. Georgia quit her job as an elementary schoolteacher and sank into a deep depression, which she medicated with alcohol.

Georgia's children tried to help, to no avail. When she arrived at a family dinner intoxicated, they took away her car keys. After a few months of chauffeuring her, her eldest son, Robert, invited her to move in with his family, but she declined. Her daughter Ginny offered to help her choose an assisted living facility. She flatly refused to leave her home. Then Sparkle, Georgia's terrier, ran away and turned up at the home of her youngest son, Daniel. When he tried to return the dog, she told him to keep her.

Georgia's children became estranged. Not even her friends from church desired her company. Her pastor ceased to visit, and her name was expunged from the rolls.

You found out about Georgia while attending a social gathering of the Women's Society. When you heard two of Georgia's friends speak of her desperate situation, you offered to accompany them on a visit. One offered to make a casserole, and the other would bring flowers from her garden.

The three of you walked up a path bordered by an overgrown lawn and untended hedges. You stood on the veranda and knocked. Then one of the women peered in a window. Through a torn shade, she saw that Georgia had fallen. You called 911.

At the hospital, the emergency physician determined that Georgia had died two days before, when she had fallen and hit her head on a coffee table. An autopsy revealed that she would have soon died of diseases related to alcoholism.

Scripture

Luke 6:43-45

No good tree bears bad fruit, nor again does a bad tree bear good fruit; for each tree is known by its own fruit. Figs are not gathered from thorns, nor are grapes picked from a bramble bush. The good person out of the good treasure of the heart produces good, and the evil person out of evil treasure produces evil; for it is out of the abundance of the heart that the mouth speaks.

Sermon

Jesus was a perceptive judge of character. He knew who would follow him when he asked them to come, such as Matthew and James. He knew who was too preoccupied with wealth to follow him, such as the rich young ruler. As he was dying on the cross, he asked John, whom he loved, to care for his mother Mary.

This scripture passage is part of a sermon to his disciples. It includes the beatitudes, an exhortation to love one's enemies, and a prohibition against judging others. In this part of the sermon, Jesus makes a distinction between good people and bad people. Good people come from good parents; bad people from bad parents. That is simple, but profound.

Georgia was a good person. She raised a fine family. She was devoted to her husband. She was strict but kind in the classroom. She knew how to bring out the best in her students, how to inspire them to sing with passion and precision. At her concerts, parents and neighbors sat shoulder-to-shoulder in the school gymnasium, applauding until their hands smarted.

Georgia's sons and daughter are highly accomplished. Robert is an aeronautics engineer. Ginny is a nurse practitioner. Daniel is a fitness trainer and a volunteer firefighter. All of them shared their mother's reverence for education, with their father's encouragement. Each of them has married and is raising children. Until recently, the family has gathered at least once per month to celebrate birthdays and holidays.

When their father died, the family times diminished. The gatherings were fewer. At school, Georgia became inconsolable, and her students struggled to understand. Finally, unable to continue teaching, Georgia resigned. She did not attend her retirement party. She spent that evening at home, soothing herself with alcohol.

Georgia had thrived as a leader in the community. She had created excitement and delight. When the only man she had ever loved died, she was awash in tears and angry at God. Her depression became unbearable.

Her children made every effort to help Georgia grow through her disappointment. They invited her on Sunday drives, trips to parks, family vacations. They renewed celebrations of birthdays and holidays. For Georgia, the gatherings were cheerless without her husband. She ceased to attend.

Ginny, Robert, and Daniel visited their mother. They encouraged her to participate in life again. They suggested doctors, counselors, even treatment. They realized that their mother was beyond their help. Finally, exhausted, they lost hope.

The day the paramedics arrived, they found Georgia's Bible on an end table, open to Luke 6:21, "Blessed are you who weep now, for you will laugh." Even if we abandon God, God refuses to abandon us. God has invited Georgia's soul back from whence it came. God has reunited her with her beloved husband. God has turned her mourning into dancing. God has wiped away her every tear.

Now we have memories and sadness. We have each other for support. We have the mind of Christ, which will guide us to one another's homes and to the church, where hope may be cherished. And on the day when our salvation is fully realized, we hope to be reunited with all of those whom we have loved, and heaven will rejoice.

Prayer

Almighty God,
we feel the sadness of loss.
We turn to you for solace.
Give us hope, which,
like sunlight through the leaves of a tree,
warms and guides our steps. Amen.

Graveside Prayer

Gracious God,
you are all power and wisdom and love.
Nurture us through all of our days
that we may grasp others' hands
and gaze into their eyes
and nourish them with courage. Amen.

Scripture Index